Daily Prayers & Blessings

Publications International, Ltd.

Make This Day Meaningful

Carpe diem! Seize the day! This became the cry of a group of young men at a boys' school in the 1989 movie *Dead Poets Society*. Ever since the introduction of that Latin phrase into mainstream culture, it's not uncommon to hear it—or even use it ourselves. "Carpe diem!" we may quip to our friends and family as we delve into some new experience or try something that's out of our comfort zone.

Seize the day! Embrace the gift of life! Make the most of each moment! It's a rousing and inspiring sentiment. But after that rallying cry, how do we actually make it happen? How do we go about consistently taking hold of each day in a way that is meaningful and lasting? After all, if we're going to be honest, there are times when life gets us down. During those times we may feel more like sleeping through the day than seizing it.

Daily Prayers and Blessings is a wonderful, practical means of getting your focus going in the right direction as you start each day. It can give you a lift in the thick of things or even help as you debrief at the end of your day in preparation for the next. Each day's reading provides a brief prayer that begins a conversation with God. Prayers range from praise and thanksgiving, to confession of need, to questions and concerns. They include both poetry and prose and reflect a wide range of emotions, situations, and experiences—the ups and downs we encounter along this road of life. Accompanying most prayers are short, related Bible passages for personal reflection or memorization.

Maybe you're wondering, "how does spending time in prayer help me make the most of each day?" That's a great question! Jesus extends an amazing invitation to us with these words: "Come unto me, all ye that labour and are heavy laden, and I will give you rest. Take my yoke upon you, and learn of me; for I am meek and lowly in heart: and ye shall find rest unto your souls. For my yoke is easy, and my burden is light." (Matthew 11:28–30). It's the Lord himself who invites us into an ongoing relationship, who calls us to a life of prayer!

The reality of being merely mortal and living in an often-difficult world is that *only* when we are truly rested and peace-filled can we face life with steady optimism and joy, making the most of opportunities that come our way. And it's *only* when we spend time in prayer—unloading our burdens and receiving God's rest and strength—that our hands are finally free to seize the good things God is holding out to us.

Jesus said, "I am come that they might have life" (John 10:10). When we see the reality of our spiritual need and answer Jesus' call to come to him, we're on our way to a truly abundant life. In prayer, we unburden ourselves of the weight of the world, while receiving in return the "light yoke" of his peace, his comfort, his very presence with us.

Daily Prayers and Blessings can help lead you into that place of prayer, that place of rest, that place of abundant life that Jesus promises to those who come to him.

Pick up this little volume and take time to pray today. *Carpe diem!* Seize the day! Live abundantly!

January

January 1

---

*"It is of the Lord's mercies that we are not consumed,
because his compassions fail not.
They are new every morning: great is thy faithfulness."*

Lamentations 3:22–23

The calendar is as bare as the Christmas tree. The page of tomorrow is clean and ready. May God bless the New Year that beckons. May we face what we must, celebrate every triumph we can, and make the changes we need. And now let us celebrate to the fullest this whistle-blowing, toast-raising moment, for it is the threshold between the old and new us.

January 2

---

*Restore unto me the joy of thy salvation; and
uphold me with thy free spirit.*

Psalm 51:12

The past, O God of yesterdays, todays, and
promise-filled tomorrows, can be an anchor or a
launching pad. It's sometimes easy to look back on
the pain and hurt and believe the future may be an
instant replay. Help us to accept the aches of the
past and put them in perspective, so we can also see
the many ways you supported and nurtured us.
Then, believing in your promise of regeneration, let
us meet the future free and excited to live in joy.

January 3

Therefore if any man be in Christ, he is a new creature: old things are passed away; behold, all things are become new.

2 Corinthians 5:17

O Lord, the best thing about the New Year is the word new! All the resolutions I make are meaningless unless I am truly new from the inside out. Give me a new attitude, Lord! A new focus, a new passion, a new mission— all based on the new things you want to do through me this year.

January 4

Gracious and healing God, thank you for everything you have done for me in the past.

You have restored me in unexpected ways and I will never be the same.

Thank you for being with me in the present and for the bright future you have planned for me. I pray for those who don't know you yet, who don't understand how you bless them again and again.

I will share the gratitude I feel, that others may grow to know you and your power.

In the name of Jesus, who healed the sick and made the lame to walk, I pray.

Amen.

January 5

And the eyes of them that see shall not be dim, and the ears of
them that hear shall hearken.
The heart also of the rash shall understand knowledge, and
the tongue of the stammerer shall be ready to speak plainly.

Isaiah 32:3–4

Give us eyes with which to see, noses with which to sniff, ears with which to hear the faintest sound along the paths you have set for us, O God of Daily Joys. Following you is a whole experience—body, mind, and soul.

January 6

I will praise thee, O Lord, with my whole heart; I will shew forth all thy marvellous works.

Psalm 9:1

Lord, this year I pray I will stop taking all your miraculous works for granted. Whether I praise you through songs, words, or actions, I want to praise you not only for what you are doing, but also for all you have done in the past. Help me see the holiness of the ordinary in each day of this New Year.

January 7

Trust in the Lord with all thine heart;
and lean not unto thine own understanding.
In all thy ways acknowledge him, and he shall direct thy paths.

Proverbs 3:5–6

I can look over my shoulder and see times when you, Pathfinding God, were a ready and dependable companion. I couldn't have done it without you. And I believe that you are already waiting to take my hand into tomorrow—knowledge that gives me the security to take risks.

January 8

The Lord is my rock, and my fortress, and my deliverer; my God, my strength, in whom I will trust; my buckler, and the horn of my salvation, and my high tower.

Psalm 18:2

*L*ord, you are the foundation of my life. When circumstances shift and make my world unsteady, you remain firm. When threats of what lies ahead blow against the framework of my thoughts, you are solid. When I focus on your steadfastness, I realize that you are my strength for the moment, the one sure thing in my life. Because of you I stand now, and I will stand tomorrow as well, because you are there already. Amen.

January 9

For sin shall not have dominion over you: for ye are not under the law, but under grace.

Romans 6:14

Every day I blow it. Every day I need your grace, Lord. I am thankful that it isn't necessary to live a perfect life to have access to your grace. If that were the case, I'd be in big trouble. But instead of turning your back on me when I veer from your paths, you are always ready to welcome me with open arms. You simply call me to trust in your saving, relationship-restoring grace. That's where I'm standing right now—in that amazing grace of yours, asking you to forgive and restore me once again so I can resume good fellowship with you.

January 10

But the fruit of the Spirit is love, joy, peace,
longsuffering, gentleness, goodness, faith,
Meekness, temperance: against such there is no law.

Galatians 5:22–23

Thank you, Father, for your Holy Spirit, who guides me through each day. Help me to obey quickly when I am asked to serve or forgive others. May I always be thankful and rejoice in the blessings pointed out to me along the way.

January 11

Not rendering evil for evil, or railing for railing: but contrariwise blessing; knowing that ye are thereunto called, that ye should inherit a blessing.

1 Peter 3:9

Let's revive the custom of blessing. When we bless someone, we show love and respect. Sincerely honoring the people and things in our lives is a wonderful way of showing gratitude to the Lord.

January 12

---

*He causeth the grass to grow for the cattle, and herb for the
service of man: that he may bring forth food out of the earth;
And wine that maketh glad the heart of man, and oil to make
his face to shine, and bread which strengtheneth man's heart.*

Psalm 104:14–15

Lord, each day you furnish us with our daily bread. You
feed and nourish us, yet often we neglect to acknowledge
your gifts of food.

Forgive us, Father, for our selfishness and our disregard
for your faithful care. We know that prayer should be a
necessary part of every meal.

If, in our haste, we forget to thank you, Lord, remind us of
our rudeness. Our meals are not complete until we thank
the giver for his many gifts.

January 13

A friend loveth at all times, and a brother is born for adversity.

Proverbs 17:17

People can often sense when someone is in need of prayer—even if that someone is miles away. If the thought of a friend should come into your mind, why not stop and say a little prayer on their behalf?

January 14

Rejoice in the Lord always: and again I say, Rejoice.

Philippians 4:4

Lord, you are the source of all joy! Regardless of how happy we may feel at any given time, we know happiness is fleeting. Happiness, so dependent on temporary circumstances, is fickle and unpredictable. But joy in you is forever! And so we come to you today, Lord, rejoicing in all you were, all you are, and all you will ever be. Because of you, we rejoice!

January 15

How great are his signs! and how mighty are his wonders! his kingdom is an everlasting kingdom, and his dominion is from generation to generation.

Daniel 4:3

Regardless of what the future holds, I'm savoring all sorts of wondrous things I've been too busy to notice before. A thousand daily marvels bring a smile to my face. Through your grace, Lord, rather than thinking how sad it is that I missed them before, I'm delighted to be seeing and doing them now. These small wonders energize me, and for that I'm thankful. It's never too late to be a joyful explorer.

January 16

Lead me in thy truth, and teach me: for thou art the
God of my salvation; on thee do I wait all the day.

Psalm 25:5

Life has made the most hopeful among us skeptical, Lord
of truth. Much is bogus, making us uncertain. Thank you
for the gift of doubt, for it sparks our seeking. Keep us
lively and excited as we set off on quests blessed by you,
heeding your advice to knock, seek, and ask.

January 17

I long to help every needy person in the world, Lord. Perhaps the most effective way to do this is by praying that you will send help wherever it is needed. Meanwhile, there is my corner of the universe with its many needs. Some of these are surely within my reach: half of my sandwich to the person standing near the freeway ramp with a sign; an evening spent going through my closet and setting aside items to donate; a weekend afternoon of helping with events at my church; a monthly visit to the sick, homebound, or imprisoned. It's a privilege to honor you by extending your compassion—in person.

January 18

Who is he that condemneth? It is Christ that died, yea rather, that is risen again, who is even at the right hand of God, who also maketh intercession for us.

Romans 8:34

Lord, how unworthy we feel of your son's prayers on our behalf, but how grateful we are for his intercession! It's all more marvelous, more mysterious than we can grasp, but because we trust your Word and your heart, we humbly thank him for caring so much about us. Surely his prayers are heard above all others!

January 19

Heal me, O Lord, and I shall be healed; save me,
and I shall be saved: for thou art my praise.

Jeremiah 17:14

*L*ord, bless all those today who need healing of any kind. Whether it be physical, emotional, or mental, bless them with your merciful grace and eternal love. Let each one know that they are special in your eyes and that, in the realm of spirit, there is only perfection, wholeness, and joy. Amen.

January 20

Whosoever therefore shall humble himself as this little child,
the same is greatest in the kingdom of heaven.

Matthew 18:4

Bless the children, God of little ones, with their giggles and wide-eyed awe, their assumption that today will be chock-full of surprises, learning, and love. Neither missing nor wasting a minute, they take nothing for granted. Their example blesses us. We will go and do likewise.

January 21

---

*Wherefore, if God so clothe the grass of the field, which to
day is, and to morrow is cast into the oven, shall he not
much more clothe you, O ye of little faith?
Therefore take no thought, saying, What shall we eat? or,
What shall we drink? or, Wherewithal shall we be clothed?*

Matthew 6:30-31

If I count the things I've asked for that you
have not given me, I begin to believe you do not
love me, God. But if, instead, I bring to mind all
of the goodness you have shown me, I come to
trust that you have never given me less than
what I need and often have blessed me with far
more from a depth of love I cannot comprehend.

January 22

For I know the thoughts that I think toward
you, saith the Lord, thoughts of peace, and
not of evil, to give you an expected end.

Jeremiah 29:11

Lord, how it must amuse you at times to see us
orchestrating the details of our days as if everything
and everyone were in our control. It's only when you
are involved in our plans that things go smoothly,
Lord. Teach us to trust that your way is the better
way, even when we can't see how every detail will
turn out. Our insight is only as good as our reliance
on you. Please be with us each day, Lord.

January 23

Then hear thou from the heavens, even from thy dwelling place, their prayer and their supplications, and maintain their cause, and forgive thy people which have sinned against thee.

2 Chronicles 6:39

God, I do not intend to hurt you and others. I am not always sure what happens in those times when I do hurt you and others. I am thankful that you forgive. Please help others to forgive me, too. Remind us all to follow your teachings. We pray that you will guide and comfort us.

January 24

And there ye shall eat before the Lord your God, and ye shall rejoice in all that ye put your hand unto, ye and your households, wherein the Lord thy God hath blessed thee.

Deuteronomy 12:7

May you find joy and satisfaction in your family life. In building a home and setting up a residence—be blessed! In finding a job and working diligently—be blessed! In taking care of little ones and making friends in the neighborhood—be blessed! In seeking God for all your help and guidance, bringing every care to him, yes, may you indeed be blessed.

January 25

Lord, we are so thankful to you for our families and close friends. How lonely our lives would be without them, even in this splendid world of your making! What a privilege it is to come to you every day to offer prayers for them. Day after day I bring before you those close to me who need your special attention. If I can't sleep at night, I pray for them again. Each one is so precious to me, Lord, and I know you cherish them as well. As I think of them during the day, please consider each thought to be another small prayer.

January 26

---

*And the Lord God formed man of the dust of
the ground, and breathed into his nostrils the
breath of life; and man became a living soul.*

Genesis 2:7

Lord, with each breath I take I am aware that
it is you who breathed life into me. My next
breath is as dependent on you as my last
breath was. And I can confidently rest in the
knowledge that it will be you and you alone
who will determine when the last breath
leaves my body and I go to be with you. Today,
Lord, I thank you for the gift of life and for
each breath I take.

January 27

Blessed is every one that feareth the Lord;
that walketh in his ways.
For thou shalt eat the labour of thine hands:
happy shalt thou be, and it shall be well with thee.

Psalm 128:1–2

Join us at work, Lord, and in our insecurities about it;
getting to and from it; in our triumphs and masteries
over it; and short cuts and temptations through it.
Work, amazingly, is where we spend most of our time.

January 28

But seek ye first the kingdom of God, and his righteousness;
and all these things shall be added unto you.
Take therefore no thought for the morrow: for the morrow
shall take thought for the things of itself.

Matthew 6:33–34

I'm getting a crick in my neck trying to see around the bend, God of past and future. I'm wearing myself out second guessing. Teach me to live in today, needing just a small glimpse down the road. No need to borrow trouble that may not be waiting.

January 29

And walk in love, as Christ also hath loved us,
and hath given himself for us an offering and a
sacrifice to God for a sweetsmelling savour.

Ephesians 5:2

God, you gave up your own beloved son for
me. How could I possibly love with such a
sense of sacrifice? Help me be the kind of
person who can put the needs of others
before my own. Help me give until it hurts.
You have sacrificed for me—now let me give
of myself in return. I know that in the end, I
will be rewarded with your merciful grace.
Amen.

January 30

Let us therefore come boldly unto the throne of grace, that we may obtain mercy, and find grace to help in time of need.

Hebrews 4:16

Everything looks much brighter than it did before. My prayer for strength has been answered. My cries for help have been heard. My pleas for mercy flew directly to your throne. Now I'm ready to help my neighbor, Lord. Let me not delay.

January 31

And I will bring the blind by a way that they knew not; I will lead them in paths that they have not known: I will make darkness light before them, and crooked things straight. These things will I do unto them, and not forsake them.

Isaiah 42:16

Lord, how grateful I am that you are willing to go before me to prepare the way. Even when I sense that a new opportunity is from you and has your blessing, I've learned I still need to stop and ask you to lead before I take the first step. Otherwise I will stumble along in the dark tripping over stones of my own creation! Everything goes more smoothly when you are involved, Lord.

February

February 1

I will open rivers in high places, and fountains in the midst of the valleys: I will make the wilderness a pool of water, and the dry land springs of water.

Isaiah 41:18

Moms know what to make from hamburger, fabric scraps, and winter: meatloaf, quilts, and windowsill gardens! As God does, they show their children how to live "as if." As if useless can become useful, as if seemingly dead can live, as if spring will come.

February 2

Thou madest him to have dominion over the works of thy hands:
thou hast put all things under his feet:
All sheep and oxen, yea, and the beasts of the field;
The fowl of the air, and the fish of the sea, and whatsoever
passeth through the paths of the seas.

Psalm 8:6–8

Winters can be long, Lord, as I've complained before, and hope elusive. Thank you for sending me outdoors. My spirit soars at the sight of a woodchuck waking from winter sleep. I rub sleep from my eyes, grateful for signposts of change, like pawprints in the mud, leading me to springs of the soul.

February 3

If any of you lack wisdom, let him ask of God, that giveth to all men liberally, and upbraideth not; and it shall be given him.

James 1:5

Thank you for your wise ways, Lord. Following them fills my life with true blessings—the riches of love and relationship, joy and provision, peace and protection. I remember reading in your Word that whenever I ask for your wisdom from a faith-filled heart, you will give it, no holds barred. So I'll ask once again today for your insight and understanding as I build, using your blueprints.

February 4

---

*Be careful for nothing; but in every thing by
prayer and supplication with thanksgiving let
your requests be made known unto God.*

Philippians 4:6

Prayer, O God, is as steadying as a hand on the rudder of
a free-floating boat and as reliable as sunrise after night. It
keeps me going, connected as I am to you, the source of
wind beneath my daily wings.

February 5

But godliness with contentment is great gain.

1 Timothy 6:6

I celebrate the gift of contentment, knowing there is no guarantee it will last. But for now, it's great to rest—just rest—in this wonderful calm.

February 6

Thy word is a lamp unto my feet, and a light unto my path.

Psalm 119:105

Lord, in your infinite wisdom you knew we would need instruction for life, and so you placed in your Word the guidelines for living a productive life that brings you glory. Your Word nurtures us body and soul and keeps our minds focused on the beautiful, positive aspects of life. Thank you, Lord, for not leaving us here without a guidebook. We'd be lost without your Word.

February 7

Praise ye the Lord. Praise God in his sanctuary: praise him in the firmament of his power. Praise him for his mighty acts: praise him according to his excellent greatness.

Psalm 150:1–2

Lord, how we want to run to you in times of need—and how blessed we are that we always find you available. You always take us in and calm our weary spirits. You, O Lord, are mighty and unchangeable! At times when everything seems shaky and uncertain, you are firm and immovable. We praise you, Lord!

February 8

Hast thou not known? hast thou not heard, that the everlasting God, the Lord, the Creator of the ends of the earth, fainteth not, neither is weary? there is no searching of his understanding.

Isaiah 40:28

To embrace the gifts each day brings is to acknowledge that the Creator never walks away from his creation. Rather, his hand is always at work making us better than we know we can be.

February 9

Now faith is the substance of things hoped for, the evidence of things not seen.

Hebrews 11:1

God of my life, though you are not visible to me, I see evidence of your existence everywhere I look. You speak to me in silent ways with an inaudible voice. How can I explain this mystery—what I know to be true but cannot prove? This spiritual sensitivity—this awareness of you—is more real to me than the pages on which my eyes fall at this moment. You exist, and I believe.

February 10

When we think of joy, we often think of things that are new—a new day, a new baby, a new love, a new beginning, the promise of a new home with God in heaven. Rejoicing in these things comes from having joy in the God who makes all things new. The scriptures command us not to rely on earthly pleasures, but to rejoice in God and in each new day he brings. Joy is a celebration of the heart that goes beyond circumstances to the knowledge that we are loved by God.

February 11

And why beholdest thou the mote that is in thy brother's eye,
but considerest not the beam that is in thine own eye?

Matthew 7:3

Lord, it is tempting and easy to cast a scornful
eye on those around us and note every fault.
When my pride tempts me to do so, prompt me
to turn the magnifying glass on myself instead.
If I keep in mind how much I need your
forgiveness every day, my love for you will
never grow cold. I know you are willing to
forgive each and every fault if I only ask.

February 12

For I am persuaded that neither death, nor life, nor angels, nor principalities, nor powers, nor things present, nor things to come, Nor height, nor depth, nor any other creature, shall be able to separate us from the love of God, which is in Christ Jesus our Lord.

Romans 8:38–39

May you come to know that God is your friend. When you feel a frowning face is looking down at you from heaven, recall that nothing you could do could ever make God love you more or love you less. He simply loves—completely, perfectly. So feel the blessedness of that!

February 13

And be not conformed to this world: but be ye transformed by the renewing of your mind, that ye may prove what is that good, and acceptable, and perfect, will of God.

Romans 12:2

What a day. When all else fails, rearrange the furniture. Lend a shoulder, God of change, as I scoot the couch to a new spot. Like a wanderer looking for your promised land, I need a fresh perspective. My life has turned topsy-turvy, and I need a new place to sit, first with you, then with the rest of my world. I need to be prepared for whatever happens next, and nothing says it like a redone room. I smile as I take my new seat; this is a better view.

February 14

Judge not, and ye shall not be judged: condemn not, and ye shall not be condemned: forgive, and ye shall be forgiven.

Luke 6:37

I pray, Lord, for the ability to learn forgiveness. Often within my heart there is much that is negative. I pray to learn to let go of those feelings. I pray to learn to forgive others as I wish to be forgiven. I pray for the gifts of understanding and compassion as I strive to be more like you. Amen.

February 15

Hear me when I call, O God of my righteousness:
thou hast enlarged me when I was in distress;
have mercy upon me, and hear my prayer.

Psalm 4:1

Lord, maybe it's during the times we aren't sure
you are hearing our prayers that we learn to trust
you the most. Eventually—in your time—we hear
your answer. We know that you are still sovereign,
and all our hopes and dreams are safe in your
hands. Even when the answer to a prayer is "no,"
we are comforted by the knowledge that you care
about us and respond to our concerns in a way
that will ultimately be for our good.

February 16

Now we have received, not the spirit of the world,
but the spirit which is of God; that we might know
the things that are freely given to us of God.

1 Corinthians 2:12

Open up my heavy heart,

That surely day by day,

The bitterness and wrath in me

Will slowly drain away.

God let your spirit enter in

And fill each empty space

With peace and healing to my soul

Through your unending grace.

February 17

And these all, having obtained a good report through
faith, received not the promise:
God having provided some better thing for us, that they
without us should not be made perfect.

Hebrews 11:39–40

Although our eyes should always be turned upward toward God, sometimes we can do with a reminder of God's work just a little bit closer to home. The faith of others can serve as a reminder or an inspiration to strengthen our own faith. Just as we should provide encouragement to others, we can also draw on others to help steady ourselves.

February 18

Save me, O God; for the waters are come in unto my soul.

Psalm 69:1

Just when all seems hopeless, prayer lifts us like a boat on an ocean wave. A sturdy craft, prayer doesn't hide from pain, but uses it like the force of the sea to move us to a new place of insight, patience, courage, and sympathy. Always, it is God's hand beneath the surface holding us up.

February 19

For so is the will of God, that with well doing ye may put to silence the ignorance of foolish men: As free, and not using your liberty for a cloak of maliciousness, but as the servants of God.

1 Peter 2:15–16

I feel free in your love, God. I feel as if I can live free from others' opinions, free from guilt, and free from fear because no matter what, your love is there for me. But I know that freedom can be abused, so help me remember that I also have been freed from the tyranny of hatred and arrogance. Help me exercise self-discipline so that I do not enslave myself to foolish extremes you never intended for me. Show me how to remain free and to lead others into your sanctuary of peace and freedom. Amen.

February 20

---

*I will praise the name of God with a song, and
will magnify him with thanksgiving.*

Psalm 69:30

Cherish the chance to work and play and think and speak
and sing; all simple pleasures are opportunities for
grateful praise.

February 21

Thou art wearied in the greatness of thy way; yet saidst thou not, There is no hope: thou hast found the life of thine hand; therefore thou wast not grieved.

Isaiah 57:10

Lord, today my heart goes out to all those whose past mistakes weigh them down and make any vision they have of their future dreary at best. Oh, that they might know you and the saving grace you bring! Draw near to them today, Lord. Reveal yourself to them in a way that will reach them, and through your mercy and forgiveness, bestow upon them a new vision—a new hope.

February 22

All scripture is given by inspiration of God, and is profitable for doctrine, for reproof, for correction, for instruction in righteousness: That the man of God may be perfect, thoroughly furnished unto all good works.

2 Timothy 3:16–17

Father, your Word makes it clear to me that the life of faith is not passive. While we wait for you to answer prayer, grant wisdom, and open doors, we also keep our minds sharp and our hearts strengthened by reading and studying your Word, by meeting with you in prayer, and by finding encouragement among other believers. These are the disciplines our souls need to stay focused on ever-present hope.

February 23

And he shall be like a tree planted by the rivers of water, that bringeth forth his fruit in his season; his leaf also shall not wither; and whatsoever he doeth shall prosper.

Psalm 1:3

The older I get, the more aware I am of the seasons of life, Lord. I know that when we draw our energy and resources from your living Word, we truly can be compared to the trees that thrive near streams of water. The fruit of a young life lived for you may look a bit different than the fruit visible in the lives of older folks, but it all brings you glory. Thank you, Lord, for supplying your living water through all the seasons of our lives. Without it, we could bear no worthy fruit at all.

February 24

Now there are diversities of gifts, but the same Spirit.

1 Corinthians 12:4

Help me take stock of your gifts to me, Lord. I'm good at things that appear to be so insignificant. Chances are you can use any one of these gifts, no matter how simple they appear, to help others. Remind me that it's not what I do but my doing it that ultimately matters.

February 25

*Pleasant words are as an honeycomb, sweet
to the soul, and health to the bones.*

Proverbs 16:24

The best medicine for a discouraged spirit is a dose of
love. Add a touch of support from friends and family,
mix with a pinch of awareness of God's presence, and
spread over your entire heart and soul. Wait ten
seconds, then smile. Nothing can withstand such a
powerful healing balm.

February 26

———◆———

But I say unto you, Love your enemies, bless them that curse you, do good to them that hate you, and pray for them which despitefully use you, and persecute you.

Matthew 5:44

Heavenly Father, give us the forgiving spirit we so badly need to heal the wounds of the past. Help us live "the better life" by making peace with our enemies and understanding that they, too, need your love. Amen.

February 27

But now the Lord my God hath given me rest on every side, so that there is neither adversary nor evil occurrent.

1 Kings 5:4

You, O Lord, are our refuge. When the days are too full and sleep is hard to come by, we simply need to escape to a quiet place and call on you. In your presence we find strength for our work and peace for our troubled minds. We are grateful for the comfort of your embrace, Lord.

February 28

For by grace are ye saved through faith; and that not of
yourselves: it is the gift of God:
Not of works, lest any man should boast.

Ephesians 2:8–9

Lord, I am grateful that you don't have a list of criteria for being eligible for salvation. What insecurity that would create in us! I feel blessed that I don't need to resort to servile fear or self-important boasting when it comes to my standing with you. Your salvation is a gift available to all and secured by your merits (not mine). It is received only by grace through faith in you.

March

March 1

Wherefore comfort yourselves together, and edify one another, even as also ye do.

1 Thessalonians 5:11

Bless those who mentor, model, and cheer me on, Lord, urging me toward goals I set, applauding as I reach them, and nourishing me to try again when I don't. Remind me to be a cheerleader. I plan to say thanks to those who are mine.

March 2

> *He maketh the storm a calm,*
> *so that the waves thereof are still.*
> *Then are they glad because they be quiet; so he*
> *bringeth them unto their desired haven.*
>
> **Psalm 107:29–30**

Sometimes my heart is so overwhelmed, God, that I don't know where to begin my prayer. Help me to quiet my soul and remember that you know everything inside of my mind before I ever come to you with it. Still, I need to tell you about it, Lord, and I know you want me to tell you. Thank you for being such a faithful listener and for caring about everything that concerns me. When I remember that, it helps me slow down, take a deep breath, and begin the conversation.

March 3

Feed the flock of God which is among you, taking the oversight thereof, not by constraint, but willingly; not for filthy lucre, but of a ready mind; Neither as being lords over God's heritage, but being examples to the flock.

1 Peter 5:2–3

Father, help us to touch and influence others. We want them to recognize and celebrate even the small blessings. We want to surprise them with gestures of love. Amen.

March 4

Owe no man any thing, but to love one another: for he that
loveth another hath fulfilled the law.

Romans 13:8

May you enjoy all the streams of love that flow into your
life: the love from family and friends; the love from
parents and children; the love from pets and the love from
God. Celebrate love all day long. For it is the breath of your
existence, and the best of all reasons for living.

March 5

The Lord our God be with us, as he was with our fathers: let him not leave us, nor forsake us.

1 Kings 8:57

*L*ife becomes much easier and more enjoyable when we know we are never alone. We always have our Higher Power to turn to for strength, hope, guidance, and renewal. God is on the job 24 hours a day, 7 days a week, 365 days a year.

March 6

Now the God of hope fill you with all joy and peace in believing, that ye may abound in hope, through the power of the Holy Ghost.

Romans 15:13

*L*ord, help me remember that you are the God of hope. You don't want me to feel sad or hopeless. It isn't your plan for me to live in fear or doubt. Help me to feel and access the power of the Holy Spirit. I know that through your Spirit I will find the hope and joy and peace you have promised to your people.

March 7

*Even so ye, forasmuch as ye are zealous of spiritual gifts, seek
that ye may excel to the edifying of the church.*

1 Corinthians 14:12

Inspired by you, Great God, and grateful for the unique
gifts we're discovering, we toss ourselves into the stream
of life to make ripples wherever we are. In your hands, our
gifts can offer a gift that keeps on making ever-widening
circles to reach all those stranded on the shore.

March 8

*Let your conversation be without covetousness; and
be content with such things as ye have: for he hath
said, I will never leave thee, nor forsake thee.*

Hebrews 13:5

*L*ord, what comfort we find in your changeless
nature. When we look back and remember all the
ways you've guided us in the past, we know we
have no need to be anxious about the future. You
were, are, and always will be our Savior and Lord.
Why should we fear instability when you are
always here with us?

March 9

For as the earth bringeth forth her bud, and as the garden causeth the things that are sown in it to spring forth; so the Lord God will cause righteousness and praise to spring forth before all the nations.

Isaiah 61:11

It's easy to praise you for your majesty and power when we see thundering waterfalls, crashing ocean waves, or majestic sunsets. Help us learn to praise you when we see a dewdrop, a seedling, or an ant.

March 10

Cast thy burden upon the Lord, and he shall sustain thee: he shall never suffer the righteous to be moved.

Psalm 55:22

Lord, I know you will show your goodness and faithfulness to me if I just diligently seek you. The problem isn't your willingness to give, but my tendency to try to do everything by myself rather than leaning on and trusting in you. This silly inclination brings me needless stress and wastes precious time. Today I endeavor to lay my needs and troubles at your feet the minute I begin to feel the least bit overwhelmed.

March 11

---

*Wherefore, my beloved brethren, let every man be swift to hear,
slow to speak, slow to wrath:
For the wrath of man worketh not the righteousness of God.*

James 1:19–20

Father God, we know that to receive the blessing
of healing, the heart must be open. But when we
are mad, we close off the heart as if it were a
prison. Remind us that a heart that is shut cannot
receive understanding, acceptance, and renewal.
Even though we feel angry, we must keep the
heart's door slightly ajar so your grace can enter
and fill our darkness with the light of hope.

March 12

God is our refuge and strength, a very present help in trouble.

Psalm 46:1

Lord, we understand that there are and will be problems in our lives, but please remind us of your presence when the problems seem insurmountable. We want to believe that you know best. We hope to remain patient as we search for purpose. Amen.

March 13

For we know that if our earthly house of this tabernacle were dissolved, we have a building of God, an house not made with hands, eternal in the heavens.

2 Corinthians 5:1

Lord, how hopelessly aware we are of our earthly bodies. They develop creaks and frailties—not to mention weird bumps and lumps! But thanks to you, we are so much more than our bodies. For although we live in the flesh, we are filled with your Holy Spirit; the life we live is really you living out your life in us! Thank you for that perspective, Lord. It makes it so much easier to watch our earthly bodies begin to fail. How ready we will be to exchange them for the heavenly models!

March 14

———◆———

*Thy faithfulness is unto all generations: thou hast
established the earth, and it abideth.*

Psalm 119:90

Human faith lives between two extremes, Lord.
It's neither completely blind nor able to see
everything. It has plenty of evidence when it steps
out and trusts you, but it takes each step with a good
many questions still unanswered. It's really quite an
adventure, this life of faith. And Lord, I must confess
that experiencing your faithfulness over time makes
it easier and easier to trust you with the unknown in
life. Thank you for your unshakable devotion.

March 15

But let patience have her perfect work, that ye may be perfect and entire, wanting nothing.

James 1:4

O Lord, what a comfort it is to know that you are working to perfect us even on days when we feel anything but perfect. One day all creation will be perfected. How we look forward to that day when our faith is fully realized, and we are complete in you!

March 16

*And we have known and believed the love that
God hath to us. God is love; and he that dwelleth
in love dwelleth in God, and God in him.*

1 John 4:16

Love. It seems so simple. Love is a gift given. Yet, if
we don't overlook it, Lord, we treat it like a gift
certificate saved so long it expires. We are down-on-
our-knees grateful your gifts of love and grace never
expire. Nudge us to use them, for we lose their value
each day they go unclaimed. We stay disconnected
from you, the one source of all creation. To connect
only requires a "Yes!" from us. Hear us shout!

March 17

I am Alpha and Omega, the beginning and the ending, saith the Lord, which is, and which was, and which is to come, the Almighty.

Revelation 1:8

*L*ord, you know all things, from beginning to end, for you are the eternal, all-knowing God. I don't need to fear what is yet to come because I belong to you, and you have given me the gift of eternal life. I come to you today to be refreshed by your presence and your Word.

March 18

How can I rejoice when I'm having "one of those days," Father? How can I pray continually when I feel overwhelmed?

When I look to Jesus' example, I find the answers I seek. He didn't stay on his knees all the time, but he did maintain an ongoing dialogue with you. He acknowledged that he would prefer to avoid his cross, but he willingly took it up because it was necessary. He focused on the joy to come later, in due time.

I too can give thanks for the good things in my life, even when bad things are bearing down on me. I can keep up a dialogue with you as I go about my day, and I can be joyful in a deep abiding sense, knowing that all is in your hands.

March 19

Rejoice evermore.
Pray without ceasing.
In every thing give thanks: for this is the
will of God in Christ Jesus concerning you.

1 Thessalonians 5:16–18

Bless me with silent conversations, O God, so I may be with you while doing chores, while singing in the shower, while brushing the cat. Sometimes words don't have to be spoken to be understood, and I get your message, too, in the silence that fills and comforts.

March 20

And the peace of God, which passeth all understanding, shall keep your hearts and minds through Christ Jesus.

Philippians 4:7

Lord, even though I know worry is a useless waste of time and energy, it snares me again and again. Thank you for helping me notice early on that I'm about to wallow in worry once more. As I give this situation to you, Lord, I release my need to worry about it as well. Instead, I look for the blessings in the midst of all that's going on and thank you wholeheartedly for them. I willingly trade my worry for your peace.

March 21

Thou hast turned for me my mourning into dancing: thou hast put off my sackcloth, and girded me with gladness.

Psalm 30:11

Security, loving God, is going to sleep in the assurance that you know our hearts before we speak and are waiting, as soon as you hear from us, to transform our concerns into hope and action, our loneliness into companionship, and our despair into dance.

March 22

---

*For when God made promise to Abraham, because he could
swear by no greater, he sware by himself,
Saying, Surely blessing I will bless thee, and multiplying I will
multiply thee.*

Hebrews 6:13–14

Faith in a wise and trustworthy God, even in broken
times like these, teaches us a new math: subtracting old
ways and adding new thoughts because sharing with
God divides our troubles and multiplies unfathomable
possibilities for renewed life.

March 23

I have gone astray like a lost sheep; seek thy servant; for I do not forget thy commandments.

Psalm 119:176

Dear Lord, when I am sad, you give me hope. When I am lost, you offer me direction and guidance. When I am alone, you stand beside me. When my heart aches with sorrow, you bring me new blessings. Thank you for your gifts of grace, love, and healing. Amen.

March 24

But it is good for me to draw near to God: I have put my trust in the Lord God, that I may declare all thy works.

Psalm 73:28

Because God is good, he loves to bless us. Yet his deepest longing is for a relationship with us. As you enjoy the good things the heavenly Father has given to you, take time to commune with him, to grow closer to him, and to get to know him a little better.

March 25

The Lord hath appeared of old unto me, saying, Yea, I have loved thee with an everlasting love: therefore with lovingkindness have I drawn thee.

Jeremiah 31:3

Lord, you have seen the times when I've been abandoned by those in whose love I have trusted. You have known the loneliness in my soul. I must confess to you that it causes me to wonder if your love has failed me, too. I need you to assure me that you are still here and that you will always stay with me.

March 26

And the fruit of righteousness is sown
in peace of them that make peace.

James 3:18

Kindness sows a seed within me that begins to sprout where before all was barren. Leaves of trust start to bud, and I branch out. I take in gentle caring and loving nudging and realize I might just go ahead and bloom! After all, God arranged spring after winter.

March 27

Greater love hath no man than this, that a man lay down his life for his friends.

John 15:13

When I think about your example of love, dear God, I realize that love is far more than a warm emotion. It is a deep commitment to look out for another's best interest, even at one's own expense. Please teach me to put my pride and my heart on the line. Please protect me, Lord, as I love others in your name. Amen.

March 28

That being justified by his grace, we should be made heirs according to the hope of eternal life.

Titus 3:7

Lord, I do believe! And because of my hope for life with you in eternity, there is all the more meaning for life today. There's meaning in my choices, my relationships, my work, my play, my worship. It all matters, it all counts, and I live knowing one day I'll stand in your presence with great joy.

March 29

Humble yourselves therefore under the mighty hand of God, that he may exalt you in due time.

1 Peter 5:6

We become discouraged when we try to live according to our own time clocks. We want what we want, and we want it this very minute. Then, when we don't get it, we sink in the quicksand of hopelessness and defeat. Only when we realize that God is at work in our lives will we begin to relax and let things happen in due season. Fruit will not ripen any faster because we demand it. It will ripen in all its sweet splendor when it is ready in spite of our demands.

March 30

Finally, brethren, whatsoever things are true, whatsoever things are honest, whatsoever things are just, whatsoever things are pure, whatsoever things are lovely, whatsoever things are of good report; if there be any virtue, and if there be any praise, think on these things.

Philippians 4:8

*L*ord, so often we find ourselves asking you to save us from bad situations only to discover you quietly revealing to us that we are our own worst enemies! Teach us to break destructive habits and to stop polluting our minds with negative thoughts, Lord. Save us from our enemies, even when it means you have to step in and save us from ourselves!

March 31

For thou hast made him most blessed for ever: thou hast made
him exceeding glad with thy countenance.

Psalm 21:6

Lord, I open my eyes and all I see are the amazing blessings that surround me. In this moment, I want for nothing, and I live with the knowledge that I can always turn to you for help, and cast my cares upon you, when my clarity and my vision cloud with worry. Thank you, Lord, for reminding me that the joyful blessings of this moment are all because of your love for me.

April

April 1

Then shall the virgin rejoice in the dance, both young men and old together: for I will turn their mourning into joy, and will comfort them, and make them rejoice from their sorrow.

Jeremiah 31:13

Father, you will help us to survive the seasons of surprises in our lives. For just as the harshest winter always gives way to the warm blush of spring, the season of our suffering will give way to a brighter tomorrow, where change becomes a catalyst for new growth and spiritual maturity. Amen.

April 2

And it came to pass in those days, that he went out into a
mountain to pray, and continued all night in prayer to God.

Luke 6:12

A sturdy bridge, prayer connects us to you, God, and you
are always first to celebrate our joys and first to weep at
our troubles. It is in this sharing that love brings about its
most miraculous ways, and we are lifted above the trials
and tribulations of life. Thank you, Lord.

April 3

Thou shalt surely give him, and thine own heart shall not be grieved when thou givest unto him: because that for this thing the Lord thy God shall bless thee in all thy works, and in all that thou puttest thine hand unto.

Deuteronomy 15:10

Heavenly Father, just for today, please keep my eyes open, my hands willing, and my heart eager to help everyone in need who crosses my path. Please do this even if the need is as small as an encouraging smile or if the need requires a sacrifice of time and talent. Just for today, God. With your guidance, I have faith that, day by day, I can help more and give more.

April 4

Ointment and perfume rejoice the heart: so doth the sweetness of a man's friend by hearty counsel.

Proverbs 27:9

A healthy friendship enhances our lives. What a blessing to have someone who wants to share all our joys and sorrows. We should continually strive to be the kind of friend God would like us to be—and the kind of friend that we would like to have.

April 5

Be still, and know that I am God: I will be exalted among the heathen, I will be exalted in the earth.

Psalm 46:10

*L*ord, it often happens that you are trying to communicate an important truth to us, but we are so busy searching for the truth elsewhere that we don't stop and listen. Teach us the importance of being still, Lord. Only when we are still can we be aware of your presence and hear your voice. Only when we quiet the stirrings of our own souls can we connect with your will! Speak to us, Lord—and help us be ready to listen.

April 6

He hath made every thing beautiful in his time: also he hath set the world in their heart, so that no man can find out the work that God maketh from the beginning to the end.

Ecclesiastes 3:11

Change is inevitable, Lord, we know. Help us accept this. If we view each transition as an opportunity to experience your faithfulness, we make new places in our lives for spiritual growth.

April 7

Delight thyself also in the Lord: and he shall give thee the desires of thine heart.

Psalm 37:4

Lord, I'm glad that the more I give, the more you give. Reward me for the risks I take on your behalf. Amen.

April 8

He that is of a proud heart stirreth up strife: but he that putteth his trust in the Lord shall be made fat.

Proverbs 28:25

Lord, we live in a world where there is a great clamoring for power and glory. Greed runs rampant, and time and again we see the inglorious results of someone's unethical attempts to climb to the top. Protect us from such fruitless ambition, Lord. For we know that it is only when we humble ourselves that you will lift us up higher than we could ever have imagined. All power and glory is yours, forever and ever. Until we acknowledge that truth, we will never be great in anyone's eyes—especially yours.

April 9

Lay not up for yourselves treasures upon earth, where moth and rust doth corrupt, and where thieves break through and steal: But lay up for yourselves treasures in heaven, where neither moth nor rust doth corrupt, and where thieves do not break through nor steal.

Matthew 6:19–20

O Lord, how many distractions there are in this world! How easy it is for us to get caught up in the desire to acquire, moving from one purchase to the next. How tempting to read one self-help book after another, until we are dizzy. Lord, I know that true contentment, true beauty, and true wisdom are all found only in your Word. Protect me from focusing too much on material things.

April 10

The Lord is my shepherd; I shall not want. He maketh me to lie down in green pastures: he leadeth me beside the still waters.

Psalm 23:1–2

Lord, bring me to the place where peace flows like a river, where soft green grasses gently hold the weight of my tired body, where the light of a new sunrise casts warmth.

April 11

And there shall be a tabernacle for a shadow in the day time from the heat, and for a place of refuge, and for a covert from storm and from rain.

Isaiah 4:6

We are grateful, O God, for your steadfastness. Thank you for showing us how, during raging winds, the mother cardinal refuses to move, standing like a mighty shelter over the fledglings beneath her wings. Secure us in the truth that we, the children of your heart, are likewise watched over and protected during life's storms.

April 12

Commit thy way unto the Lord; trust also in him; and he shall bring it to pass.

Psalm 37:5

Father, there are many events in our lives over which we have no control. However, we do have a choice either to endure trying times or to give up. Remind us that the secret of survival is remembering that our hope is in your fairness, goodness, and justice. When we put our trust in you who cannot fail us, we can remain faithful. Our trust and faithfulness produce the endurance that sees us through the tough times we all face in this life. Please help us to remember. Amen.

April 13

Then was our mouth filled with laughter, and our tongue with singing: then said they among the heathen, The Lord hath done great things for them.

Psalm 126:2

Inspired by you, O God, I wisely invest in the future by deciding to chase kites on spring days, to chase balls on playgrounds, and to chase laughter rising from a baby's lips like bubbles on the wind rather than to chase dust bunnies beneath beds! Amen.

April 14

So then faith cometh by hearing, and hearing by the word of God.

Romans 10:17

Lord, I want my thoughts to be like your thoughts. I want to discern what you discern and have the insight you have into all that happens in the world. I know that can never really be, Lord, but if I am open to your Spirit at all times, perhaps I can construe your hopes now and then. May my mind never be so cluttered that I fail to receive a message you are trying to share with me, Lord.

April 15

---

*And the bow shall be in the cloud; and I will look upon it, that
I may remember the everlasting covenant between God and
every living creature of all flesh that is upon the earth.*

Genesis 9:16

Refocus me, God of love, to embrace and enjoy this child
growing so quickly into independence. When growth pains
come, send me a rainbow of friends' support, vision, and
patience to enjoy, although it's sure to rain again. Help me
accept storm and sun as the balance of nature and of life.

April 16

The grace of the Lord Jesus Christ, and the love of God, and the communion of the Holy Ghost, be with you all. Amen.

2 Corinthians 13:14

Like sun that melts the snow,

my soul absorbs the grace

that beats in gentle, healing rays

from some godly place.

Like rain that heals parched earth,

my body drinks the love

that falls in gently soothing waves

from heaven up above.

April 17

I sought the Lord, and he heard me, and
delivered me from all my fears.

Psalm 34:4

No matter the worries I have, small or large, you, O God, are there ahead of me with promises of help and support that relieve me and free me from getting stuck in the mire of my daily fears. I am grateful.

April 18

———————

*Blessed are the peacemakers: for they
shall be called the children of God.*

Matthew 5:9

Father, you are the greatest of all peacemakers.
You made reconciliation with humanity possible by
means of great personal sacrifice yet without
compromising the truth. Show me how to follow
your example today. Help me not to settle for fake
peace—the kind that comes when lies are allowed
to prevail for the sake of avoiding conflict. Instead,
grant me the courage, grace, and wisdom to work
toward real peace, which values all people and
fulfills our need for truth and love.

April 19

And my people shall dwell in a peaceable habitation, and in sure dwellings, and in quiet resting places.

Isaiah 32:18

O Holy Creator, who hath bound together heaven and earth, let me walk through your kingdom comforted and protected by the warm rays of your love. Let me be healed as I stand basking in the divine light of your presence, where strength and hope and joy are found. Let me sit at rest in the valley of your peace, surrounded by the fortress of your loving care.

April 20

---

*To every thing there is a season, and a time to
every purpose under the heaven.*

Ecclesiastes 3:1

How certain the seasons are, Lord! How faithfully you
usher them in one after the other, each in its assigned
order. The spring has come with its rains once again, just
as I knew it would. And spring's arrival reminds me that
you—the faithful creator—have promised to dwell with
those who long to know you, those who search for you and
look for your return.

April 21

For, lo, he that formeth the mountains, and createth the wind,
and declareth unto man what is his thought, that maketh the
morning darkness, and treadeth upon the high places of the
earth, The Lord, The God of hosts, is his name.

Amos 4:13

Lord, we praise you for all the beauty and wonder you've placed in the world. How creative of you to think of a creature as exuberant and joyful as the hummingbird! How interesting that you sprinkled spots on the backs of the newborn fawns that follow along behind their mother through our backyard. Let us never become so accustomed to your glorious creation that we take it for granted, Lord. You've blessed us with a wonderland, and we thank you for it.

April 22

Verily I say unto you, Whosoever shall not receive the kingdom of God as a little child, he shall not enter therein. And he took them up in his arms, put his hands upon them, and blessed them.

Mark 10:15–16

O Lord, what a blessing children are in this world. They bring such joy into our lives and are a precious composite of the best of our past and the hopes for the future. Thank you for your love for all children, Lord. Please guard them always.

April 23

I have made the earth, and created man upon it: I, even my hands, have stretched out the heavens, and all their host have I commanded.

Isaiah 45:12

What "speaks" to you in nature? The amazing variety of birds coming and going at your bird feeder? The petals on those wildflowers by your mailbox? The smell of the air after a rainstorm? The night sky? Maybe you simply wonder how those weeds can find a way to thrive in the cracks of the sidewalk. Whatever impresses us among the things God has made, it's a part of his messaging system to us, inviting us to search him out and find relationship with him.

April 24

Thou wilt shew me the path of life: in thy presence is fulness of joy; at thy right hand there are pleasures for evermore.

Psalm 16:11

God, shine your healing light down upon me today, for my path is filled with painful obstacles and my suffering fogs my vision. Clear the challenges from the road I must walk upon, or at least walk with me as I confront them. With you, I know I can endure anything. With you, I know I can make it through to the other side, where joy awaits. Amen.

April 25

And thou shalt be secure, because there is hope; yea, thou shalt dig about thee, and thou shalt take thy rest in safety.

Job 11:18

Almighty God, I know you are supremely faithful! Today I ask you to restore hope to the hopeless. Plant seeds of hope in hearts that have lain fallow for so long. Send down showers of hope on those struggling with illness, persecution, or difficult relationships. Hope that comes from you is hope with the power to sustain us when nothing around us seems the least bit hopeful.

April 26

As every man hath received the gift, even so minister the same one to another, as good stewards of the manifold grace of God.

1 Peter 4:10

Please let me help you

however I can.

Long ages ago

it was God's plan

for me to serve,

to love, and to share,

helping ease another's

burden of care.

So let me be

God's loving gift to you

because in serving others,

I am blessed, too.

April 27

For, brethren, ye have been called unto liberty; only use not liberty for an occasion to the flesh, but by love serve one another.

Galatians 5:13

Be ready to offer your gentle touch today—and celebrate the gift of kindness. Reach out to the elderly and infirm. Stretch out your hand to the children and infants. Do not hold back. Celebrate by letting your warmth flow through. And rejoice in your ability to do God's will in this way.

April 28

According as his divine power hath given unto us all things that pertain unto life and godliness, through the knowledge of him that hath called us to glory and virtue.

2 Peter 1:3

Father God, you are the giver of all gifts. All of our resources and all we have came from you, and they are only ours for a little while. Protect us from any addiction to material things, Lord. Gently remind us when we have enough—enough to eat, enough to wear, enough to enjoy. Most of all, keep us mindful of the fact that because we have you, we have everything we need.

April 29

He hath shewed thee, O man, what is good; and what doth the Lord require of thee, but to do justly, and to love mercy, and to walk humbly with thy God?

Micah 6:8

I am here right now, Father, because I do want to walk in your ways. I know the key is staying connected to you because the ways of the world are all around me, always imposing a different set of values and a different worldview. Give me a wise and discerning heart in all things today so I can stay on track.

April 30

Even there shall thy hand lead me,
and thy right hand shall hold me.

Psalm 139:10

I see a robin's egg hatching, Lord, and am set free
from my doubts and fretting. For, while life is not
always filled with joy and happiness, I know it is always
held in your hand.

May 1

Let all those that seek thee rejoice and be glad in thee: and let
such as love thy salvation say continually, Let God be magnified.

Psalm 70:4

As we learn to trust you, God, we discover your
strengthening presence in various places and
people. Wherever we encounter shelter, comfort,
rest, and peace, we are bound to hear your voice,
welcoming us. And in whomever we find truth,
love, gentleness, and humility, we are sure to hear
your heartbeat, assuring us that you will always be
near. Thank you, God. Amen.

May 2

For the invisible things of him from the creation of the world are clearly seen, being understood by the things that are made, even his eternal power and Godhead; so that they are without excuse.

Romans 1:20

God, you are invisible but not unseen. You reveal yourself in creation and demonstrate your kindness in a stranger's sincere smile. You are intangible but not unfelt. You caress our faces with the wind and embrace us in a friend's arms. We look for you and feel your presence. Amen.

May 3

Herein is my Father glorified, that ye bear
much fruit; so shall ye be my disciples.

John 15:8

Lord, how I pray that your love is evident in me today!
I want to follow you closely and help draw others to you
as well. I know that if those with whom I come in
contact see love, joy, peace, patience, kindness,
goodness, faithfulness, gentleness, and self-control in
me, they may find you as well. Direct my steps as I
follow you, Lord, and may the grace you've sprinkled on
me be revealed for your glory. Amen.

May 4

Casting all your care upon him; for he careth for you.

1 Peter 5:7

When trouble strikes, we're restored by the smallest gestures from God's ambassadors: friends, random kindnesses, shared pain and support, even a stranger's outstretched hand. And we get the message: God cares.

May 5

Through the tender mercy of our God; whereby the dayspring
from on high hath visited us,
To give light to them that sit in darkness and in the shadow of
death, to guide our feet into the way of peace.

Luke 1:78–79

No matter how deep a rut we dig ourselves into, the arms of God are long enough to lift us up into a newer life free from struggle. No matter how dark a tunnel we crawl into, the love of God is strong enough to reach in and guide us toward a brighter life, free from fear.

May 6

And ye shall be hated of all men for my name's sake: but he that endureth to the end shall be saved.

Matthew 10:22

*L*ord, how I long to stand strong in the faith! I read of the martyrs of old and question my own loyalty and courage. Would I, if my life hung in the balance, say, "Yes, I believe in God"? I pray I would, Lord. Continue to prepare me for any opportunity to stand firm for what I know to be true. To live without conviction is hardly to live at all.

May 7

For thou art my lamp, O Lord: and the
Lord will lighten my darkness.

2 Samuel 22:29

Heavenly Father, I ask for your bright presence. Protect me from the worldly hurts and evils that sometimes cloud life and rob me of joy. Help me forget the past, look to the future, and be eager for new starts. Replace darkness, doubt, and sorrow, and replace it with the light of your love. Forgive me, so I might forgive others. Amen.

May 8

I will instruct thee and teach thee in the way which thou shalt go: I will guide thee with mine eye.

Psalm 32:8

Help me be open to your guidance, Lord, however it comes. When you speak to me in the words of a friend, open my ears. When you touch me in the embrace of a family member, let me feel your gentle touch. And when you come to me in the almost imperceptible rush of angels' wings, alert my senses to your presence.

May 9

For thou art great, and doest
wondrous things: thou art God alone.

Psalm 86:10

My Creator, blessed is your presence. For you
and you alone give me power to walk through
dark valleys into the light again. You and you
alone give me hope when there seems no end to
my suffering. You and you alone give me peace
when the noise of my life overwhelms me. I ask
that you give this same power, hope, and peace
to all who know discouragement, that they, too,
may be emboldened and renewed by your
everlasting love. Amen.

May 10

Let us lift up our heart with our hands unto God in the heavens.

Lamentations 3:41

Lord of my heart, give me a refreshing drink from the fountains of your love, walking through this desert as I have. Lord of my heart, spread out before me a new vision of your goodness, locked into this dull routine as I was. Lord of my heart, lift up a shining awareness of your will and purpose, awash in doubts and fears though I be.

May 11

---

*And he answering said, Thou shalt love the Lord thy God with
all thy heart, and with all thy soul, and with all thy strength,
and with all thy mind; and thy neighbour as thyself.*

Luke 10:27

*O*God, your love is so great. I'm not sure that I can love as
you do or even love others in a way that will please you.
God, teach me how to really love my family, my friends,
and even strangers. I trust in the power of your love to
make me into a far more loving person than I am today.
Amen.

May 12

Abide in me, and I in you. As the branch cannot
bear fruit of itself, except it abide in the vine; no
more can ye, except ye abide in me.

John 15:4

Lord, I deeply desire to abide in you. I desire to
have you abiding in me as well, so closely that I
can speak to you any time and feel your presence.
Destroy the distractions that create distance
between us, Lord. Clear out the clutter that keeps
me from sensing your best plan for my life. Then
when I ask for what I wish, it will be the
fulfillment of your desire for me as well.

May 13

O God of justice, we confess that we are too quick at times to judge those around us, basing our opinions not upon what is written in their hearts but what is easily seen by our lazy eyes. Keep us faithful to challenge one another any time we find ourselves speaking in generalities about any group of people or repeating jokes and slurs that offend and degrade. Remind us that all of creation bears the imprint of your face, all people are children of yours, all souls are illuminated by your divine spark. We know that whatever diminishes others diminishes your spirit at work in them. Make us respectful, humble, and open to the diversity around us that reflects your divine imagination and creativity.

May 14

If we confess our sins, he is faithful and just to forgive us our sins, and to cleanse us from all unrighteousness.

1 John 1:9

Lord, it's hard for me to conceive of how thoroughly you forgive me when I confess my sins to you. The stains on my soul are washed away, and you give me a fresh, clean start. Even though it's hard for me to wrap my understanding around this, please help me wrap my faith around it so I can believe that you completely forgive me.

May 15

No man hath seen God at any time. If we love one another,
God dwelleth in us, and his love is perfected in us.

1 John 4:12

O Lord, your gift of love is often distorted in this world of ours. You are the source of the only perfect love we will ever know. Thank you, Lord, for abiding in us and helping

us love ourselves and others. On this day, Lord, I pray that you will draw near to anyone who is feeling unloved. May they accept your unconditional love so they will know what true love is!

May 16

And he said unto them, Why are ye troubled? and why do thoughts arise in your hearts?

Luke 24:38

Sometimes my doubts are so strong and so bothersome. Give me courage to express my doubts to you, O God, knowing that they are necessary moments through which I can pass on my way to true contentment in you.

May 17

He appointed the moon for seasons:
the sun knoweth his going down.

Psalm 104:19

I am grateful, God of Hope, for the gift of each new day, each new season, like the one unfolding around me now in flower and birdsong, in seedling and bud. When they arrive as surely as dawn follows night and bloom follows bulb, I am uplifted by the fulfillment of your promise.

May 18

The Lord recompense thy work, and a full reward be given thee of the Lord God of Israel, under whose wings thou art come to trust.

Ruth 2:12

Today I am tired, Lord. There seem to be too many things on my to-do list and too few hours in the day. And still, I know what a blessing it is to have work to do and to live a purpose-filled life. Thank you for tasks large and small that give meaning to our days, Lord. May we always do each one as if we were doing it only for you. And may we never assume we can do anything without your direction and energy.

May 19

*We are troubled on every side, yet not distressed; we are perplexed, but not in despair;
Persecuted, but not forsaken; cast down, but not destroyed.*

2 Corinthians 4:8–9

Lord, today I pray for all those who are in desperate need of help in order to survive: victims of earthquakes and tornadoes, the homeless, and the physically and emotionally destitute people of our world. Make yourself known to them, Lord. May they all see that their true help comes only from you! You who created them will not leave them without help, nor without hope.

May 20

---

*And the work of righteousness shall be peace; and the effect of
righteousness quietness and assurance for ever.*

Isaiah 32:17

Lord, how grateful we are for the rest you bring to
even the most harried souls. The young soldier on the
battlefield knows that peace, and so does the young
mother with many mouths to feed but too little money
in her bank account. You are the one who brings us to
the place of restoration in our hearts and minds, Lord.
Thank you for being our shepherd.

May 21

---

*Behold, I will do a new thing; now it shall spring
forth; shall ye not know it? I will even make a way in
the wilderness, and rivers in the desert.*

Isaiah 43:19

Enliven my imagination, God of new life, so that I can
see through today's troubles to coming newness.
Surround me with your caring so that I can live as if the
new has already begun.

May 22

But the scripture hath concluded all under sin,
that the promise by faith of Jesus Christ might
be given to them that believe.

Galatians 3:22

Lord, today I want to praise you for giving me the faith to believe, for faith itself is a gift from you. I lift up to you today all those I know who are having trouble accepting your gift of salvation. Be patient with them, Lord. Reveal yourself to them in a way that will reach them, and draw them into a relationship with you. Our lives are incomplete without you, Lord. Send your grace to those who are struggling.

May 23

And he saith unto them, Why are ye fearful, O ye of little faith? Then he arose, and rebuked the winds and the sea; and there was a great calm.

Matthew 8:26

Touch and calm my turbulent emotions, God of the still waters. Whisper words to the listening ears of my soul. In hearing your voice, give me assurance beyond a shadow of a doubt that you are my companion in life, eternally.

May 24

The Lord hath heard my supplication;
the Lord will receive my prayer.

Psalm 6:9

Lord, we've tossed our prayers aloft, and hopefully, expectantly, we wait for your answers. As we do, we will: listen, for you speak in the voice of nature; see you as a companion in the face and hand of a friend; feel you as a sweet-smelling rain. We feel your presence.

May 25

The Lord is my strength and song, and he is become my salvation: he is my God, and I will prepare him an habitation; my father's God, and I will exalt him.

Exodus 15:2

Dear Father God, you sent your son to us to be our Lord, to watch over us, to bring us comfort, strength, hope, and

healing, when our hearts are broken and our lives seem shattered. We will never be alone, not when you are here with us always and forever. Remind us to look to you for strength. Amen.

May 26

---

*And let us not be weary in well doing: for in
due season we shall reap, if we faint not.*

Galatians 6:9

Lord, you are the light I follow down this long, dark
tunnel. You are the voice that whispers, urging me
onward when this wall of sorrow seems
insurmountable. You are the hand that reaches out
and grabs mine when I feel as if I'm sinking in
despair. You alone, Lord, are the waters that fill me
when I am dried of all hope and faith. I thank you,
Lord, for although I may feel like giving up, you have
not given up on me. Amen.

May 27

Comfort ye, comfort ye my people, saith your God.

Isaiah 40:1

Lord, on days when everything seems to go wrong, help me to remember that you are always nearby to offer comfort. It is easy to get overwhelmed and feel lost and alone in this world, but deep down I know that is never the case. You are always at the ready to help—I just need to remember to take a moment to stop, breathe, and pray.

May 28

Wealth gotten by vanity shall be diminished: but he that gathereth by labour shall increase.

Proverbs 13:11

I thank you for my work, Lord. And please bless me in it. Most of all, help me to remember that the paycheck worth working for consists of more than just money. It must include meaning and significance, for myself and others.

May 29

But I will sacrifice unto thee with the voice of thanksgiving; I will pay that that I have vowed. Salvation is of the Lord.

Jonah 2:9

Sacrifice doesn't always come easily, Lord. Please show me those opportunities you have placed in my day for me to lay down my own to-do list and be aware of the greater things you are doing through me. Don't let me miss those opportunities, Lord. Please do not allow any grumbling on my part to deter your work. Grant me the grace to make any sacrifices you need from me today.

May 30

Jesus answered and said unto him, Verily, verily, I say unto thee,
Except a man be born again, he cannot see the kingdom of God.

John 3:3

Spiritual birth is amazing, Father! It's a miracle no less exciting than the birth of a baby. Your Word says that it causes even the angels in heaven to rejoice. Thank you for my own spiritual birth. It's the reason I'm praying right now and enjoying this fellowship with you. It's so good to be your child. Today I'll just bask in that reality.

May 31

I do set my bow in the cloud, and it shall be for a token of a covenant between me and the earth.

Genesis 9:13

God gave the rainbow as a sign of his promise to never flood the entire earth again. The colors that spread out in spectrum, as sunlight passes through water droplets in the sky, speak of God's faithfulness in keeping his promise to Noah and to all the generations that have followed. Faithfulness marks God's character. It is who he is, through and through. Let every rainbow we see remind us of God's faithful love, and let praise flow from our hearts to the one who always keeps his promises.

June 1

---

*And the scripture was fulfilled which saith, Abraham believed
God, and it was imputed unto him for righteousness: and he
was called the Friend of God.*

James 2:23

Dear God, your love embraces me like the warmth
of the sun, and I am filled with light. Your hope
enfolds me in arms so strong, I lack for nothing. Your
grace fills me with the strength I need to move
through this day. For these gifts you give me, of
eternal love, eternal peace, and most of all, for eternal
friendship, I thank you God.

June 2

When I consider thy heavens, the work of thy fingers, the moon and the stars, which thou hast ordained; What is man, that thou art mindful of him? and the son of man, that thou visitest him?

Psalm 8:3–4

Lord, it's so easy for us to get bogged down in the details of life on this earth. But when we have the opportunity to gaze up at the stars on a clear night, it is easy to remember that there is so much more to your creation than our relatively insignificant lives. You placed the stars and know them by name, Lord, and you know us by name too. We are blessed to be even a tiny part of your magnificent creation! That you also care so deeply for us is the best gift of all.

June 3

Wherefore seeing we also are compassed about with so great a cloud of witnesses, let us lay aside every weight, and the sin which doth so easily beset us, and let us run with patience the race that is set before us.

Hebrews 12:1

Some days the race feels like a sprint, Lord, and on other days, a marathon. I want to press on, but I need you to infuse my spirit with your strength and steadfastness. I want to run and finish well. Thank you for beginning the work of faith in my life and for promising not to stop working until my faith is complete.

June 4

I am grateful that you don't require spiritual gymnastics from me when I sin, Lord. You just call me to come to you with a humble and repentant heart. In my pride I sometimes want to do something that will impress you—something that will "make up for it" somehow. But you just shake your head and keep calling me to humble myself. That often doesn't seem like enough to me. But I guess that's the point: I can never earn your grace; it is a gift. Christ died on the cross for us because it is beyond our powers to make up for all the sins we have committed. I bring my contrite heart before you now, Lord. Thank you for receiving it as an acceptable sacrifice.

June 5

I, even I, am he that blotteth out thy transgressions for mine own sake, and will not remember thy sins.

Isaiah 43:25

A chart of my efforts to change traces a jagged course, Lord, like the lines on a heart-rate monitor. Reassure me that instead of measuring my failures, I must remember that I am alive and ever-changing. Help me become consistent, but deliver me from flat lines.

June 6

The Lord will strengthen him upon the bed of languishing:
thou wilt make all his bed in his sickness.

Psalm 41:3

*L*ord, you do not leave us live our lives alone. You are with us in health, in sickness, and in every moment in between. Thank you for your comfort and constant presence. Thank you for sticking with us through the good times and the bad. Most of all, thank you for being there when we need you the most. Amen.

June 7

And let the peace of God rule in your hearts, to the which also
ye are called in one body; and be ye thankful.

Colossians 3:15

Sometimes we believe our souls can only be at peace if there is no outer turmoil. The wonder of God's peace is that even when the world around us is in confusion and our emotions are in a whirl, underneath it all we can know his peace.

June 8

For if our heart condemn us, God is greater than our heart,
and knoweth all things.

1 John 3:20

It's hard, Lord, to reveal my heart to you, though it's the thing I most want to do. Remind me in this dialogue that you already know what is within me. You wait—thank you!—hoping for the gift of my willingness to acknowledge the good you already see and the bad you've long forgotten.

June 9

There is no fear in love; but perfect love casteth out fear: because fear hath torment. He that feareth is not made perfect in love.

1 John 4:18

God of All Comfort, I know that with you by my side I am never alone. Your perfect love casts out all fear, doubt, and uncertainty. Your presence emboldens and empowers me. You are the light that leads me to safety again. Amen.

June 10

---

*And this I do for the gospel's sake, that I might
be partaker thereof with you.*

1 Corinthians 9:23

All our opportunities, abilities, and resources come
from God. They are given to us to hold in sacred trust
for him. Cooperating with God will permit us to
generously pass on to others some of the many
blessings from his rich storehouse.

June 11

He discovereth deep things out of darkness, and bringeth out to light the shadow of death.

Job 12:22

Teach us to know, God, that it is exactly at the point of our deepest despair that you are closest. For at those times we can finally admit we have wandered in the dark, without a clue. Yet you have been there with us all along. Thank you for your abiding presence.

June 12

Look upon mine affliction and my pain; and forgive all my sins.

Psalm 25:18

*L*ord, today I pray for all those who are suffering from any sort of addiction. Whether it's drugs, gambling, overeating, or compulsive exercising, Lord, addiction keeps them from being the people you designed them to be. Their obsession separates them from you and walls them off from their loved ones as well. Break through and release them from their chains, Lord. Give them the strength to put their troubles behind them and find new life in you.

June 13

And he said unto me, My grace is sufficient for thee: for my strength is made perfect in weakness. Most gladly therefore will I rather glory in my infirmities, that the power of Christ may rest upon me.

2 Corinthians 12:9

Lord, I am aware that you, by your grace, have given me the strength to work through life's challenges. I accept that when I am completely out of ideas and drained of all energy, your grace and strength lifts me up and carries me forward. Thank you, Lord.

June 14

I am Alpha and Omega, the beginning and the end, the first and the last.

Revelation 22:13

You are everywhere, Lord, and we are comforted to be enfolded as we move through our lives. You are with us in birthings and dyings, in routine and surprise, and in stillness and activity. We cannot wander so far in any direction that you are not already there.

June 15

Beloved, now are we the sons of God, and it doth not yet appear what we shall be: but we know that, when he shall appear, we shall be like him; for we shall see him as he is.

1 John 3:2

*L*ord, if my hunger and thirst for your righteousness could be satisfied by ordering from a spiritual drive-thru, I'd want to supersize my order! I so want to be like Christ. I want to have his courage and humility, his strength and gentleness. I don't want substitutes—such as pride that looks like courage or fear that looks like humility. I want the real deal. Thank you for the promise that you will satisfy this craving of mine, this deep soul hunger to be and do all that is right, true, and good.

June 16

And when we cried unto the Lord God of our fathers, the Lord heard our voice, and looked on our affliction, and our labour, and our oppression.

Deuteronomy 26:7

Praise the Lord, for he has seen the affliction and heard the groans of his people—both his children who were slaves in Egypt and those who are in bondage to physical pain. Indeed, he has come to me in my darkest moment and rescued me from my misery. He is a compassionate and wonderful God, who loves his children and watches over each one of us.

June 17

These are exciting times to be part of your world, O God, for your Spirit is stirring us into vision and action to revitalize our communities. Be with us in difficult times of decision-making. We must learn to be united, despite our differences of opinion.

Move us beyond our too-busy schedules, our boredom with routine and committees, and our preference to debate and deliberate rather than do. Be with us as we volunteer and vote. Be with and bless us, the ordinary citizens, for we are as needy as our streets and communities.

Extend your hand of grace and bless us as we revitalize our neighborhoods, communities, and country, keeping you as cornerstone and Master Builder.

June 18

But if from thence thou shalt seek the Lord thy God, thou shalt find him, if thou seek him with all thy heart and with all thy soul.

Deuteronomy 4:29

Comfort us, God, when we come to this awesome conclusion: What did not satisfy us when we finally laid hold of it was surely not the thing we were so long in seeking. Yes, comfort us by this recognition: In all our longings, we are only yearning for you.

June 19

Through faith we understand that the worlds were framed by the word of God, so that things which are seen were not made of things which do appear.

Hebrews 11:3

I can't make a blade of grass grow, Lord. By contrast, you created this entire universe and all it contains. If that doesn't inspire worship in my soul, I can't imagine what will. But the truth is that it does put me in awe of you; it does stir my heart to join in the worship of heaven.

June 20

For to be carnally minded is death; but to be spiritually minded is life and peace.

Romans 8:6

Spirit, carry me like a feather upon the current to a place of serenity. Let the waters flow over me like cleansing balm. Set me upon the dry place, where life begins anew. Spirit, carry me like a feather back home again.

June 21

Lord, if my world were turned upside down in a single day like Job's was—losing everything I owned, and far worse, all of my children being killed by a natural disaster—I doubt worship would be my instinctive response. But here is Job, recognizing himself as a mere man and praising you because you are God. He trusts your wisdom that reaches above and beyond his overwhelming tragedy. Somehow, he is able to understand that the blessings you gave him are not his to hold on to or his that he can demand repayment from you. Even Job's punishing trials could not shake his faith in you.

June 22

———◆———

Study to shew thyself approved unto God, a workman that needeth not to be ashamed, rightly dividing the word of truth.

2 Timothy 2:15

I know it is important to be physically healthy and strong, but how much the better if we're also spiritually strong! Sure, lifting weights does our bodies good, but regularly picking up a Bible is good for the health of our souls. And rather than just doing deep knee bends to increase our physical strength, we can also regularly "hit our knees" in prayer to strengthen our core spirits.

June 23

Let all bitterness, and wrath, and anger, and clamour, and evil speaking, be put away from you, with all malice.

Ephesians 4:31

God, grant me the courage to let go of shame, guilt, and anger. Free me of all negative energies, for only then will I become a conduit for joy and a channel for goodness. Amen.

June 24

———◆———

Neither yield ye your members as instruments of
unrighteousness unto sin: but yield yourselves unto God, as
those that are alive from the dead, and your members as
instruments of righteousness unto God.

Romans 6:13

*L*ord, help me to depend on you to be my source
of goodness. I don't always feel like being patient,
kind, loving, or joyful, but you are all of these
things by your very nature. So right now I place
my strengths and weaknesses into your hands,
asking you to infuse them with yourself and to
make them instruments of good that will serve
others for your sake.

June 25

Hold up my goings in thy paths, that my footsteps slip not.

Psalm 17:5

*L*ord, far too often we try to steer the course of our lives without consulting you, and we always run into problems. Set us on a true course that will bring us closer to you. Amen.

June 26

I have refrained my feet from every evil way, that I might keep thy word.

Psalm 119:101

$\mathcal{D}$ear God, help us to see that none of us are immune to losing ourselves or to hurting one another. Please help us stay on course so we may find our own true essences. Amen.

June 27

Drop down, ye heavens, from above, and let the skies pour down righteousness: let the earth open, and let them bring forth salvation, and let righteousness spring up together; I the Lord have created it.

Isaiah 45:8

Lift up your heart in sweet surrender to the God who is waiting to shower you with blessings. Lift up your soul on wings of joy to the God who is waiting to guide you from the chaos of shadows out into the light of a peace that knows no equal.

June 28

Then came Peter to him, and said, Lord, how oft shall my brother sin against me, and I forgive him? till seven times? Jesus saith unto him, I say not unto thee, Until seven times: but, Until seventy times seven.

Matthew 18:21–22

Dear God, thank you for children who teach us to be open and forgiving. Help us forgive those who hurt us so

the pain will not be passed on through the generations. Thank you for forgiving our sins and help us be at peace with our families. Amen.

June 29

Watch ye, stand fast in the faith, quit you like men, be strong.

1 Corinthians 16:13

Even in our toughest moments, Lord, we yearn to grow into fullest flower. Give us a faith as resilient and determined as dandelions pushing up through cracks in the pavement.

June 30

Judge not according to the appearance,
but judge righteous judgment.

John 7:24

I am grateful, O God, that your standards run more to how we're loving you and one another than how we appear. If you judged on lawns, I would be out in the cold!

Mine is the yard where kids gather. Ball games, sprinkler tag, snow forts, tree house constructions, car tinkerings and bike repair—they all happen here.

Bless my rutted, littered lawn, wise Creator. It's the most beautiful landscape, dotted as it is with children who will be grown and gone faster than we can say "replant."

July

July 1

Thou hast heard my voice: hide not thine ear at my breathing,
at my cry.

Lamentations 3:56

Today, heavenly Father, you may call upon me to
listen to someone and hear that person's heart. It
may be someone who needs to feel significant enough
to be heard, or perhaps someone who is lonely and
longs to be connected to another person, or maybe
someone who is hurting and needs a sympathetic ear.
Whatever the case, Lord, please open my ears so I
may listen to someone today. Amen.

July 2

———◆———

When we think of integrity, we think of someone who is honorable and trustworthy—a person who keeps their word and guards their reputation. To be called a man or woman of integrity is a high compliment. Such a person knows the difference between right and wrong and diligently pursues doing right, no matter what the obstacles. Jesus provides the best example of a man of integrity; he was not swayed by outer influences but lived a life above reproach. Integrity comes not just from the pursuit of right living, but the pursuit of God, which leads to right living. Lord, grant me integrity as I seek to follow your commands.

July 3

*Serve the Lord with gladness: come before
his presence with singing.*

Psalm 100:2

To serve means to assist or be of use. Serving is one of the reasons we are on this earth and the reason Jesus himself said he came to the earth. When we serve, we reach out to meet the needs of others; service is an outward sign that we belong to God and desire to do his will. True service is not about grudgingly doing for others because of obligation, but an act that flows willingly, as a channel for God's love. True servants give not just with their hands, but with their hearts. Heavenly Father, grant me a spirit of true service.

July 4

Stand fast therefore in the liberty wherewith Christ hath made us free, and be not entangled again with the yoke of bondage.

Galatians 5:1

I love the freedoms I enjoy as your child, Father. I also deeply appreciate the freedoms I enjoy as a citizen of a free country. Both citizenships—my heavenly one and my earthly one—call for responsible living on my part, but these responsibilities are really a joy and a privilege. Help me to always keep this in the forefront of my mind as I make choices each day.

July 5

---

*And he changeth the times and the seasons: he removeth
kings, and setteth up kings: he giveth wisdom unto the wise,
and knowledge to them that know understanding.*

Daniel 2:21

Just when I settle in with one reality, something
new disrupts it. Overnight change, God of all the time
in the world, is comforting and grief-making, for it's a
reminder that nothing stays the same. Not tough
times, not good ones either. Despite today's
annoyance, I'm grateful for change, assured it will take
me to new moments you have in mind.

July 6

For we brought nothing into this world, and it is certain we can carry nothing out.

1 Timothy 6:7

Lord God, why is it that we tend to hold so tightly to the things of this world? We know in our hearts that everything we have is ours only by your grace and great generosity. When we accumulate more than we need, it only builds barriers between ourselves and you. Thank you for your provision, Lord. May we learn to hold everything loosely, knowing it is only borrowed.

July 7

For out of much affliction and anguish of heart I wrote unto you with many tears; not that ye should be grieved, but that ye might know the love which I have more abundantly unto you.

2 Corinthians 2:4

If God has touched us with his love, the result will be love flowing through us to others. When we realize the depth of his love, our hearts long to show that kind of love to those around us.

July 8

O come, let us sing unto the Lord: let us make a joyful noise to the rock of our salvation.

Psalm 95:1

Sometimes I demand,
"God give me joy!"
and nothing happens.
Yet joy flows naturally,
lavishly,
when I seek to
know you,
love you, and
serve you.

July 9

I will extol thee, O Lord; for thou hast lifted me up, and hast not made my foes to rejoice over me.

Psalm 30:1

God, when life feels like a ride that won't let us off, remind us that you are waiting for us to reach up to you. And when we finally do, we will thank you for being there to lift us to peace and safety.

July 10

Every day will I bless thee; and I will praise thy name for ever and ever.

Psalm 145:2

The dawn of a new day brings new possibilities and challenges. We hope they'll all be good ones, but we know they won't, and that's where God comes in.

July 11

Be ye angry, and sin not: let not the sun go down upon your wrath:
Neither give place to the devil.

Ephesians 4:26–27

Heavenly Father, teach me to forgive others their transgressions and to let go of angers and resentments that poison the heart and burden the soul. Teach me to love and understand others and to accept them as they are, not as I wish they would be. Amen.

July 12

$\mathcal{I}$ want to draw closer to you, Lord, to immerse myself in your faithfulness. Getting to know you will take effort and sacrifice on my part, though, and in today's culture, time seems limited. People feel they have precious little time with family and friends; time with God seems nearly impossible. Help me to adjust my busy schedule and find creative ways to spend time with you.

I can spend time with you during my drive to work or the grocery store. I can spend time with you while I exercise or fold laundry. I can spend time with you while I take a shower or cook dinner.

I don't want to miss quality time with you, Lord, due to time constraints. Many times life is hectic and full of distractions, but I will keep my eyes focused on you and my ears ready to listen.

July 13

Let every thing that hath breath praise the Lord.
Praise ye the Lord.

Psalm 150:6

God, help me celebrate this day with all my heart, to rejoice in the beauty of its light and warmth. May I give thanks for the air and grass and sidewalks. Help me feel grateful as others flow into my soul. May I cherish the chance to work and play, to think and speak—knowing this: All simple pleasures are opportunities for praise.

July 14

Let brotherly love continue.
Be not forgetful to entertain strangers: for thereby some have
entertained angels unawares.

Hebrews 13:1–2

*L*ord, I know it isn't enough to experience love. I have to get out there in the world and do loving things as well. Help me find ways to be of service and bring more love into my life. Direct the course of my actions, and inspire me with ideas that help me, in turn, inspire others. Amen.

July 15

But they that wait upon the Lord shall renew their strength;
they shall mount up with wings as eagles; they shall run, and
not be weary; and they shall walk, and not faint.

Isaiah 40:31

Lord, let me be strong today, drawing my courage from my hope in you. Help me lean not on my own strength but on your limitless power. I know there is work to be done—burdens to be lifted, temptations to be resisted, unkindness to be forgiven. Let my thoughts and actions be motivated by the hope generated by your promises.

July 16

---

*Who comforteth us in all our tribulation, that we may be able
to comfort them which are in any trouble, by the comfort
wherewith we ourselves are comforted of God.*

2 Corinthians 1:4

God promises us his comfort, but he also uses us as his
agents to comfort others. In fact, the difficulties we've
gone through often give us the ability to reassure others
who are now going through the same experiences. God,
how can you use me today to extend comfort to
someone else?

July 17

*From the rising of the sun unto the going down of the same
the Lord's name is to be praised.*

Psalm 113:3

What a relief in this throwaway world of ever-changing values to know that you, O God, are the same yesterday, today, and tomorrow. Your trustworthiness and desire for all your children to have good things never varies. You are as sure as sunrise and sunset.

July 18

Peace is about releasing.
It's about opening my hand
and letting go of my plan,
my agenda,
my demands
on God and other people
and even on myself.
It's about realizing
that every person
is as important as I am
in God's eyes.
It's remembering
I don't know everything
and I don't have solutions
to every problem.
It's about calling on
the One who does.

July 19

And God shall wipe away all tears from their eyes; and there shall be no more death, neither sorrow, nor crying, neither shall there be any more pain: for the former things are passed away.

Revelation 21:4

I'd like to pray to be spared of all pain, but life is full of pain. No one escapes it. Better to ask God to be near whenever it comes.

July 20

And Abraham said, My son, God will provide himself a lamb
for a burnt offering: so they went both of them together.

Genesis 22:8

One of the Hebrew names for God is Jehovah Jireh. Besides having a nice ring to it, its meaning ("God, our provider") is one worth remembering. In life, we may experience times of abundance and also times when we struggle to make ends meet. In any situation, God asks us to trust and honor him as Jehovah Jireh, the God who provides all that we truly need.

July 21

And this is the confidence that we have in him, that, if we ask any thing according to his will, he heareth us.

1 John 5:14

The best listeners are often silent, the depth of their understanding revealed by their actions. God, you are one such listener. Thank you.

July 22

God thundereth marvellously with his voice; great things doeth he, which we cannot comprehend.

Job 37:5

Lord, you come to us in the storm, the fire, and even in the stillness of a quiet moment. Sometimes your message is strong, carried on bustling angelic wings; sometimes our spirits are nudged, our hearts lightened by the gentle whisper of spirit voices. However you approach us, your message is always one of tender love and compassion. Thank you for the certainty— and the surprise—of your holy voice.

July 23

Whom having not seen, ye love; in whom, though now ye see him not, yet believing, ye rejoice with joy unspeakable and full of glory.

1 Peter 1:8

*F*ather, thank you for initiating our wonderful relationship by loving me first! Your perfect love has taught me to trust you and leave my fear of your judgment behind. Your love for me brings such joy to my life, Lord. Help me spread this joy to others today.

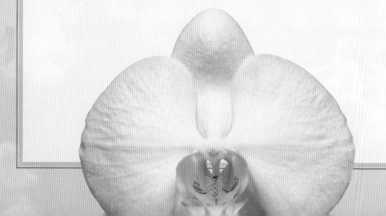

July 24

For he shall give his angels charge over thee, to keep thee in all thy ways.

Psalm 91:11

The plants breathe out and we breathe in, not noticing the exchange. And so we walk with the angels, seldom noticing the company we keep. Lord, make me aware of your presence in my life, and that of your angels.

July 25

Faith is a commodity that cannot be purchased, traded, or sold. It is a treasure that cannot be claimed and put on display in a museum. It is a richness no amount of money can compare to. When you have faith, you have a power that can change night into day, move mountains, calm stormy seas. When you have faith, you can fall over and over again, only to get up each time more determined than ever to succeed—and you will succeed. For faith is God in action, and faith is available to anyone, rich, poor, young or old, as long as you believe. Father, grant me a more perfect faith.

July 26

The thief cometh not, but for to steal, and to kill, and to destroy: I am come that they might have life, and that they might have it more abundantly.

John 10:10

Father, this morning I woke up, and the gift of life was still within me. What a privilege! I don't want to lose wonder of it for even one day. So help me to live with purpose and joy, not waiting for what today might bring me, but rather looking for opportunities to be and do all that you've created me for. And, most of all, thank you for being with me in each moment, showing me the way of abundant living.

July 27

Dost thou know when God disposed them, and caused the light of his cloud to shine?
Dost thou know the balancings of the clouds, the wondrous works of him which is perfect in knowledge?

Job 37:15–16

Nothing thrills the heart and awakens the spirit like a summer thunderstorm, alive with electric energy and thick with potential danger. With each explosive boom of thunder and blinding flash of lightning, our adrenaline rises and our hair stands on end. Without a reminder of our deep connection to the natural world, we can grow dull and lifeless, stiff and anxious, lost and uncertain. Then the thunder roars and the lightning pierces the dark sky, and we remember once again that we are all a part of something far grander and more awesome than we could ever imagine.

July 28

And this commandment have we from him, That he who loveth God love his brother also.

1 John 4:21

*L*ord, look down upon my family with merciful eyes, and help us to heal any divides that threaten to grow between us. Guide us toward solutions that will empower everyone involved, and remind us that we work better when we work together. Help us to speak honestly with each other. Amen.

July 29

Lord, what a miracle each newborn baby is. We marvel at the tiny hands and rosebud lips, and we know such a masterpiece could only come from you! We pray for all little children today, Lord. Watch over them and guide their parents. Grant all parents the courage, strength, and wisdom they need to fulfill their sacred duties.

July 30

Therefore I esteem all thy precepts concerning all things to be right; and I hate every false way.

Psalm 119:128

*L*ord, teach me to think ahead about the results my actions might inflict. If things go awry despite my forethought, help me admit my wrongs and right them. Amen.

July 31

And God made the beast of the earth after his kind, and cattle after their kind, and every thing that creepeth upon the earth after his kind: and God saw that it was good.

Genesis 1:25

God of all things, we thank you for all your creatures, from the largest to the smallest. In each of these wondrous animals, we see your creative touch. Help us  respect all you have created, to protect their lives, and to be ready to learn from them anything you would like to teach us.

August

August 1

Grace, mercy and peace from God the Father and from Jesus Christ, the Father's Son, will be with us in truth and love.

2 John 1:3

Lord, I'm glad you are merciful and gracious. Today I'm resting in your steadfast love, and in your hugs. Amen.

August 2

And I will pray the Father, and he shall give you another
Comforter, that he may abide with you for ever.

John 14:16

Dear heavenly Father, today, if I see or hear of someone
who is struggling in some way, please help me take a
moment to remember what it was like when I was
struggling and you helped me through the aid of a friend
or stranger. Let that memory mobilize me to offer help
and be your true servant. This I pray. Amen.

August 3

Blessed is the man that endureth temptation: for when he is tried, he shall receive the crown of life, which the Lord hath promised to them that love him.

James 1:12

Watching how others have coped with what's troubling us now, we take heart from their creativity, Lord, knowing you will inspire us, too, to find innovative ways to move on.

August 4

For the Lamb which is in the midst of the throne shall feed them, and shall lead them unto living fountains of waters: and God shall wipe away all tears from their eyes.

Revelation 7:17

*L*ord, how precious water is to us, and how parched and desperate we are when it's in short supply. How grateful we are that in you we have access to the living water that will never run dry! Keep us mindful of that refreshing supply today, Lord. Fill us up, for we are thirsty.

August 5

Be strong and of a good courage, fear not, nor be afraid of them: for the Lord thy God, he it is that doth go with thee; he will not fail thee, nor forsake thee.

Deuteronomy 31:6

Dear Lord, each night the news is full of trouble. So much pain and sorrow. It makes me ache to see it all. Some nights, it seems that's all there is; this world seems sometimes so weary and heavy laden. Then I turn to you and know that you are nearest on the darkest days. And there is comfort in knowing you and that you have not forsaken us or the people whose world is presently dark. Amen.

August 6

He that speaketh truth sheweth forth righteousness: but a false witness deceit.

Proverbs 12:17

I wish to be of service, Lord. So give me courage to put my own hope and despair, my own doubt and fear at the disposal of others. For how could I ever help without first being simply...real?

August 7

But the manifestation of the Spirit is given to every man to profit withal.

1 Corinthians 12:7

God, make me an open vessel through which the waters of your Spirit flow freely. Let your love move through me and out into my world, touching everyone I come in contact with. Express your joy through the special talents you have given me, that others may come to know your presence in their own lives by witnessing your presence in mine. Amen.

August 8

For the commandment is a lamp; and the law is light; and
reproofs of instruction are the way of life.

Proverbs 6:23

*L*ord, your Word is so alive and vibrant that it almost seems illuminated when I am reading it. When I am troubled, opening the Bible is like turning on a comforting light in a dark, gloomy room. Thank you, Lord, for loving us so much that you gave us your wisdom to illuminate our lives.

August 9

O give thanks unto the Lord; for he is good; for his mercy endureth for ever.

1 Chronicles 16:34

Gratitude may be the most underestimated virtue. We think of love, hope, faith, and the power of prayer and forgiveness. But how often do we stop each day and give thanks for all the blessings in our lives? Are we too focused on what we lack, what we don't have, don't want, don't need? By opening the heart and mind to focus on gratitude, we unleash a treasure of unceasing good that's just waiting to flow into our lives. A grateful person knows that by giving thanks, they're given even more to be thankful for. Holy Spirit, open my heart and mind to gratitude for your gifts.

August 10

But the Lord is my defence; and my God is the rock of my refuge.

Psalm 94:22

You are the mighty wind

that lifts me up on high

when I am weak and weary

and without the strength to fly.

You are the mighty fortress

that keeps me free from fear

and shelters me in kindness

with your tender, loving care.

August 11

Better is the end of a thing than the beginning thereof: and
the patient in spirit is better than the proud in spirit.

Ecclesiastes 7:8

Sometimes the people around me irritate me, God.
During those times, with an apology on my lips, help me
climb out of the rut of irritation and make amends. Help
me learn from my mistakes and do better. Amen.

August 12

And when the children of Israel saw it, they said one to another, It is manna: for they wist not what it was. And Moses said unto them, This is the bread which the Lord hath given you to eat.

Exodus 16:15

Bless the food I eat today. And let it remind me once again that the soul, like the body, lives and grows by everything it feeds upon. Keep me drinking only the good and the pure, for your glory. Amen.

August 13

For thy mercy is great above the heavens: and thy truth reacheth unto the clouds.

Psalm 108:4

His love is wider than our worries, longer than our loneliness, stronger than our sorrows, deeper than our doubts, and higher than our hostilities. This is why valleys are so wide, rivers so long, winds so strong, oceans so deep, and the sky is so high—with these, we can have a picture of the wonder of his love.

August 14

Till he fill thy mouth with laughing, and thy lips with rejoicing.

Job 8:21

There are broken places in our family, and it's hard, serious work patching them up. In the midst of all there is to do, we feel God leading us outdoors to splash in rains and across beaches where we are rejuvenated by the sheer pleasure of playing. Laughter, in God's splendid creation, is good for heart, mind, body, soul, and most certainly our family.

August 15

---

*For where two or three are gathered together in my name,
there am I in the midst of them.*

Matthew 18:20

*L*ord, I often pray for others when I need to pray with others. Show me the power of shared prayer as I meet with others in your name and in your presence. Amen.

August 16

And be ye kind one to another, tenderhearted, forgiving one another, even as God for Christ's sake hath forgiven you.

Ephesians 4:32

Dear heavenly Father, I truly want to do good toward others. I don't want to just talk about being good. I desire to be more compassionate. God, I need for you to teach me to be far more sensitive to the needs and sorrows of the people you have placed in my life and to be kind and encouraging toward them. I need for you to teach me how to truly love. I pray for this with all my heart. Amen.

August 17

He is like a man which built an house, and digged deep, and laid the foundation on a rock: and when the flood arose, the stream beat vehemently upon that house, and could not shake it: for it was founded upon a rock.

Luke 6:48

Dear Lord, help me to build on a firm foundation by relying on your wisdom, diligently seeking your direction in all I do, and learning to walk in your paths of kindness, peace, and justice to all those in my life. In Jesus' name, Amen.

August 18

I said, Days should speak, and multitude of years should teach wisdom.

Job 32:7

Dear God, help me see that aging, like being born, happens one day at a time. Calm my fears that it will overtake and overwhelm me. Help me briefly mourn youth as only a butterfly cocoon that must crumble to set the new creature free.

August 19

When Jesus heard it, he saith unto them, They that are whole have no need of the physician, but they that are sick: I came not to call the righteous, but sinners to repentance.

Mark 2:17

Whether we admit it or not, we all long to feel welcomed and accepted by others. Just as Jesus connected with people outside his circle of disciples, we need to connect with people outside our comfort zone and mirror God's acceptance of all people. Heavenly Father, help me reach out to all those you would put in my path.

August 20

Awake up, my glory; awake, psaltery and harp: I myself will
awake early.

Psalm 57:8

Lord, thank you for being a God of new beginnings.
Give me a fresh start today as I trust in you. Amen.

August 21

Let us come before his presence with thanksgiving, and make a joyful noise unto him with psalms.

Psalm 95:2

Lord, how blessed we are to be able to see you all around us and to sense your presence within us. Even though we can't see you in the same way we might see a friend or a neighbor, we see you in your Word and in all that is good and true in the world around us. Thank you, Lord, for making yourself so available to us.

August 22

Take fast hold of instruction; let her not go:
keep her; for she is thy life.

Proverbs 4:13

Teachers are like gardeners—planting seeds of discovery, cultivating curiosity, and nuturing the joy of learning. Lord, as another school year beckons, I thank you for all who have been good teachers to me and to the children in my life.

August 23

For if ye forgive men their trespasses, your heavenly Father will also forgive you.

Matthew 6:14

When we truly forgive those who have wronged us, we feel as light as angel's wings and as free as a child at recess. Heavenly Father, help me to forgive.

August 24

Saying with a loud voice, Worthy is the Lamb that was slain to receive power, and riches, and wisdom, and strength, and honour, and glory, and blessing.

Revelation 5:12

The light that shines upon me,

The arms that reach to hold me,

The warmth that gives me comfort,

The angel's wings that enfold me.

The word that gives me power,

The song that makes me whole,

The wisdom that empowers me,

The touch that heals my soul.

August 25

And Jesus went about all the cities and villages, teaching in their synagogues, and preaching the gospel of the kingdom, and healing every sickness and every disease among the people.

Matthew 9:35

Loving Jesus, Healer of the Sick,

I place in your hands myself and all who need your healing, in body or spirit. Help us crave the healing that only you can give. May we not define what that healing should be, but accept your gift of abundant life however you give it to us. In your way, in your time, restore us to full health and wholeness. Amen.

August 26

For the administration of this service not only supplieth the want of the saints, but is abundant also by many thanksgivings unto God.

2 Corinthians 9:12

Thank you, God, for the salesclerk who took an extra moment to be gracious, for the person who delivered my mail, and for the drivers who yielded to me without hesitation. I do not know their names, but they blessed me today with their hard work and positive attitudes.

August 27

For I say, through the grace given unto me, to every man that is among you, not to think of himself more highly than he ought to think; but to think soberly, according as God hath dealt to every man the measure of faith.

Romans 12:3

Good morning, Lord. I have another busy day ahead of me. This may be the only minute I have to talk to you. Please tap me on the shoulder now and then—no matter how busy I am—and remind me that the world does not revolve around me.

August 28

Iron sharpeneth iron; so a man sharpeneth the countenance of his friend.

Proverbs 27:17

God, you have given me friends to illuminate my path and make it smooth. They guide me when I am lost and support me when I stumble. Thank you for bringing them into my life.

August 29

And he shall be as the light of the morning, when the sun riseth, even a morning without clouds; as the tender grass springing out of the earth by clear shining after rain.

2 Samuel 23:4

With boldness and wonder and expectation, I greet you this morning, God of sunrise and rising dew. Gratefully, I look back to all that was good yesterday and in hope, face forward, ready for today.

August 30

Verily, verily, I say unto you, That ye shall weep and lament, but the world shall rejoice: and ye shall be sorrowful, but your sorrow shall be turned into joy.

John 16:20

God, thank you for sometimes reminding me that in the center of chaos lies the seed of new opportunity and that things are not always as awful as they seem at first. I often forget that what starts out bad can end up great and that it is all a matter of my own perspective. Amen.

August 31

He becometh poor that dealeth with a slack hand: but the hand of the diligent maketh rich.

Proverbs 10:4

All work can be good, Lord, for you can upgrade the most mundane, difficult, or nerve-wracking job into one that matters. God of all skills and vocations, bless and inspire my work; deliver me from boredom and laziness.

September

September 1

Henceforth I call you not servants; for the servant knoweth not what his Lord doeth: but I have called you friends; for all things that I have heard of my Father I have made known unto you.

John 15:15

Dear God, shine through me and help me lighten another's darkness by showing the same friendship that you extended. Show me a person that is in desperate need of a friend today. Help me to be sensitive, caring, and willing to go out of my way to meet this person's need right now, whether it be emotional, physical, or spiritual. Thank you that when I need a friend, you are the friend that sticketh closer than a brother. In Jesus' name, Amen.

September 2

And Sarah said, God hath made me to laugh, so that all that hear will laugh with me.

Genesis 21:6

As we face worrisome days, restore our funny bones, Lord. Humor helps rebuild and heal, sparking hope and igniting energy with which to combat stress, ease grief, and provide direction.

September 3

For ye have need of patience, that, after ye have done the will of God, ye might receive the promise.

Hebrews 10:36

O God, you have called each of us to special tasks, purposes, and vocations, equipping us with the skills and energy to perform them. For some, our vocations send us into the labor force; for some, it is soon bringing retirement. For some, it is in full-time homemaking. For some, our vocations are in artistic skills; for some, in volunteering, helping, neighboring. Always, there is that first call from you, God of vision, working through our work to help, heal, change a needful world.

September 4

God is my strength and power: and he maketh my way perfect.

2 Samuel 22:33

God is bigger than any problem you have. Whoever is opposing you is a weakling compared to God. Why not tap into God's supply of strength? Why focus on your problem when God is so much more interesting?

September 5

And forgive us our debts, as we forgive our debtors.

Matthew 6:12

*L*ord God, the words "I'm sorry" and "forgive me" have got to be the most powerful in our vocabulary. May these phrases ever be poised on my lips, ready to do their work of release and restoration. Let your healing balm wash over me, Father, as I both grant and receive the freedom that forgiveness brings. Amen.

September 6

And there are diversities of operations, but it is the same God which worketh all in all.

1 Corinthians 12:6

Father, sometimes I see people who seem to have found work perfectly suited to them, and I wonder if I am fulfilling my purpose. Thank you for reminding me that you are at work in me, bringing about your purposes, which are not always clear to me. You take even small gifts—as you did with the loaves and the fishes—and you make them multiply.

September 7

Behold, we count them happy which endure. Ye have heard of
the patience of Job, and have seen the end of the Lord; that
the Lord is very pitiful, and of tender mercy.

James 5:11

Over and over I ask myself, "What can I do?" What can I do to make a difference? One of the hardest things about reaching out is having others think I can "fix it" and then finding out that I can't. Lord, help me to remember that what you promise is not to "fix it" for us but rather to give us whatever it takes to prevail in spite of our hurts. Help me keep in mind that sometimes all that is necessary is a listening ear.

September 8

His lord said unto him, Well done, thou good and faithful servant: thou hast been faithful over a few things, I will make thee ruler over many things: enter thou into the joy of thy lord.

Matthew 25:21

*L*ord, put into my heart a pure faith that is fit for heaven.

September 9

And God blessed the seventh day, and sanctified it:
because that in it he had rested from all his work which
God created and made.

Genesis 2:3

Dear God, help us work to live instead of living just to
work. Lead us to the green pastures where we can enjoy
the companionship of our loved ones and the pleasures
that restore us. Amen.

September 10

And in every work that he began in the service of the house of God, and in the law, and in the commandments, to seek his God, he did it with all his heart, and prospered.

2 Chronicles 31:21

The angels do your work, Father. I want to do it, too. You made me a person, not an angel. I can't fly through time or travel the universe, but I am willing to do whatever I can. Help me see your agenda and stick to the plan.

September 11

And the King shall answer and say unto them, Verily I say unto you, Inasmuch as ye have done it unto one of the least of these my brethren, ye have done it unto me.

Matthew 25:40

Thank God for firefighters, for paramedics, for Red Cross teams, for police, for the National Guard, for search and rescue teams—for all who risk their lives for us, who step forward when we're hurting, who are there when we need them most.

September 12

Praise ye him, sun and moon: praise him, all ye stars of light.

Psalm 148:3

The God who hung the stars in space will turn
your darkness into light.
The God whose birds rise on the winds will give
your injured soul new flight.
The God who taught the whale its song will
cause your heart to sing again.
For the God whose power made earth and sky
will touch you with his gentle hand.

September 13

The glory of young men is their strength:
and the beauty of old men is the grey head.

Proverbs 20:29

Lord, time and again I see that you intend for the generations to go through life together. The joy the youngest child brings to the eldest grandparent is such a blessing to all who witness it. Even when it isn't possible for us all to be together all the time, let us see the wisdom in sharing our lives. Please keep us ever alert to the unique gifts each generation has to share.

September 14

---

*Thy righteousness is like the great mountains; thy judgments
are a great deep: O Lord, thou preservest man and beast.*

Psalm 36:6

Thank you, God, for all the animals who have helped us
to feel closer to you and your creation. Keep them safe,
these trusted innocents who calm our lives and show us
love. Help them find their way home if they are lost.
Help them hear the voices of those who will care for
them. Save them from every unsafe place.

September 15

I said in mine heart, God shall judge the righteous and the wicked:
for there is a time there for every purpose and for every work.

Ecclesiastes 3:17

Keep us from being slaves to time, Lord. You always create time and space for anything we are doing that brings you glory. Teach us to rest in the knowledge that time is in your hands. Whenever we think we don't have enough of it, show us you have plenty and are happy to share! Thank you, Lord, for your generous supply of time.

September 16

Hear my voice, O God, in my prayer:
preserve my life from fear of the enemy.

Psalm 64:1

God, keep me close today. Sometimes I am not at my best, and I would like someone to listen as I whine, moan, and complain. On days like that, please bear the brunt of my troubles or send someone to help in your name. Amen.

September 17

Now we exhort you, brethren, warn them that are unruly, comfort the feebleminded, support the weak, be patient toward all men.

1 Thessalonians 5:14

Thank you for those people you have sent into my life who have been angels for me. Let me find ways to be an angel for others.

September 18

Behold, I have given him for a witness to the people, a leader and commander to the people.

Isaiah 55:4

God, we know the jobs of politicians and leaders are difficult. We know they face tough decisions on a regular basis. Protect their minds, their hearts, and their souls. Thank you for the role they play in this country. Guide them in the direction that will prove best for everyone. Amen.

September 19

---

*The Lord is nigh unto them that are of a broken heart; and
saveth such as be of a contrite spirit.*

Psalm 34:18

When feelings are hurt, Wise Physician, we curl in on
ourselves like orange rinds, withholding even the
possibility of reconciliation. Help me open up to new
possibilities for righting wrong and sharing love without
reservation, as the orange blossom offers its fragrance, the
fruit of its zesty sweetness.

September 20

---

*But the men marvelled, saying, What manner of man is this,
that even the winds and the sea obey him!*

Matthew 8:27

We know you, Lord, in the changing seasons: in leaves blazing gently in fall beauty; in winter's snow sculptures. We know you in arid desert cactus blooms and in the

migrations of whales. In the blending of the seasons, we feel your renewing, steadfast care, and worries lose their power to overwhelm. The list of your hope-filled marvels is endless, our gratitude equally so.

September 21

Shew me thy ways, O Lord; teach me thy paths.

Psalm 25:4

Spirit of God, keep teaching me
the ways of change and growth.
Like the wind, you cannot be tracked or traced.
The breezes blow where they will:
silently, invisibly, with great power.
Just as you are working in lives even now.
Let me know your calling as you move in me!
Yes, whisk with your persistent prompting
through all the windows of my soul,
the dark corners of my heart.

September 22

Being filled with the fruits of righteousness, which are by Jesus Christ, unto the glory and praise of God.

Philippians 1:11

*L*ord, please help me to remember that you are the source of all good things that come out of my life as I grow and flourish in you. All the "good fruit" of love, joy, peace, patience, kindness, goodness, faithfulness, gentleness, and self-control come directly from you and then produce good things in me. I want to thank you for nourishing and supporting my life. Please use the fruit you're producing in me to nourish others and lead them to you as well.

September 23

What? know ye not that your body is the temple of the Holy Ghost which is in you, which ye have of God, and ye are not your own?

1 Corinthians 6:19

How marvelous our bodies!
May we care for them today with all the
reverence and honor we might extend
toward any great gift that defies explanation.

September 24

For my brethren and companions' sakes,
I will now say, Peace be within thee.

Psalm 122:8

Enter and bless this family, Lord, so that its circle will be
where quarrels are made up and relationships mature;
where failures are forgiven and new directions found.

September 25

But we will give ourselves continually to prayer, and to the ministry of the word.

Acts 6:4

I need to talk to you, Lord, but when and where? When life offers few prayable moments, lead me to a quiet spirit spot at work or home or in transit between the two. A brief moment is enough until we have more time.

September 26

And let it be, when these signs are come unto thee, that thou do as occasion serve thee; for God is with thee.

1 Samuel 10:7

To those scanning a night sky, you sent a star. To those tending sheep on a silent hill, you sent a voice. What sign, Lord, are you sending me to come, be, and do all you intend? Let me hear, see, and accept it when you do.

September 27

Behold, I will bring it health and cure, and I will cure them, and will reveal unto them the abundance of peace and truth.

Jeremiah 33:6

Bring your cool caress to the foreheads of those suffering fever. By your spirit, lift the spirits of the bedridden and give comfort to those in pain. Strengthen all entrusted with the care of the infirm today, and give them renewed energy for their tasks. And remind us all that heaven awaits—where we will all be whole and healthy before you, brothers and sisters forever.

September 28

Search me, O God, and know my heart: try me, and
know my thoughts:
And see if there be any wicked way in me, and lead
me in the way everlasting.

Psalm 139:23–24

Whatever is right and pure,

excellent and gracious,

admirable and beautiful,

fill my mind with these things.

Too much of the world

comes to me in tones of gray and brown.

Too great the temptation

to indulge obsessive thoughts and sordid plans.

Guard my mind; place a fence around my motives.

The pure, the lovely, the good—Yes! Only those today.

September 29

For clean air and pure water; for glorious colors in sky and tree in first and last bloom, in the wings of migrating butterfly, goose, and bird. Lord of all, to you we raise our hymn of grateful praise.

For wildlife sanctuaries, open range, prairies, mountains; for backyard gardens; for corn stalks and bean stems growing tall then bending low for harvest. For your generous gifts that meet human need. Lord of all, to you we raise our hymn of grateful praise.

Every day and night we marvel at your wondrous care. Constantly you guide our choices, inviting us to creative living. All creation reflects your empowering love: rolling countryside, majestic mountains, delicate wildflowers, and sturdy roadside blooms. Sunrise and star, warmth and chill all declare your glory, singing together. Lord of all, to you we raise our hymn of grateful praise.

September 30

For love that gives us soul-satisfying happiness; for families, friends, and all others around us; for loved ones here and loved ones beyond; for tender, peaceful thoughts. Lord of all, to you we raise our hymn of grateful praise.

For letting us know you exist through families and friends who feed us more than enough food, who give us abundant shelter and clothing, who cherish your presence and honor your creation. Lord of all, to you we raise our hymn of grateful praise.

For the pleasure of seeing your wonderful creation; for the pleasure of hearing other voices and music; for the delight of knowing and feeling; for gathering us in families and communities; for inspiring us to stretch toward new knowledge, heightened awareness; for the blending of all experience into the excitement we call life. Lord of all, to you we raise our hymn of grateful praise.

October

October 1

Great God,

I seek your wisdom and strength so that I can adapt to the changes of each new season. As the days grow shorter and the nights longer, as the warm winds give way to cool, crisp breezes, as the leaves on the trees explode in bold color, so will I give way to changes. Help me to adapt, to bend, to be flexible so that I can continue to function at my best on the inside, despite the changes going on outside of me. And as the darker days of winter loom near, let my heart be filled with only love and light and warmth for myself and for my family. And so it is.

October 2

And immediately Jesus stretched forth his hand, and caught him, and said unto him, O thou of little faith, wherefore didst thou doubt?

Matthew 14:31

Sometimes I'm like Peter, and I walk on water. I stand above my circumstances, which are like the swirling tempests of the sea. But then, like Peter, I take my eyes off Jesus and concentrate on things below. Soon I start to sink. How I long to have a consistent water-walking eyes-on-Jesus faith.

October 3

And Moses sware on that day, saying, Surely the land whereon thy feet have trodden shall be thine inheritance, and thy children's for ever, because thou hast wholly followed the Lord my God.

Joshua 14:9

We're tempted to give up until we see the geese. God provided them a "V" in which to fly, a main "point" goose providing wind resistance for followers. Geese know how to take turns naturally. When we ask for help, we too let someone else take the point position. And when we do, we feel an updraft of air to rest in, and feel God in this current of wind.

October 4

What, God of peace, are we to do with our anger when it overflows? Sometimes our anger is the only prayer we can bring you. We are relieved and grateful to know that you are sturdy enough to bear all we feel and say. Where do we go from here? What will we be without our anger when it's all that has fueled us? When we are still, we hear your answer: "Emptied." But then we would be nothing. Remind us that, in your redeeming hands, "nothing" can become of great use, as a gourd hollowed out becomes a cup or a bowl only when emptied. When the time comes for us to empty ourselves of this abundance of anger, make us into something useful. It would be a double tragedy to waste anger's re-creative energy.

October 5

Such knowledge is too wonderful for me; it is high, I
cannot attain unto it.
Whither shall I go from thy spirit? or whither shall I
flee from thy presence?

Psalm 139:6–7

Dear God,

Help my unbelief.

When I'm in pain, I forget that you care about me.

I forget that you have helped me through my trials.

I forget that you hold me in your arms to keep me safe.

I forget that you are feeling my pain with me.

I forget that you love me,

I forget that I am important to you.

Show me your presence—let me feel your enveloping love.

Heal my hurting soul.

Thank you for staying with me even in my unbelief.

Amen.

October 6

—◆—

Who his own self bare our sins in his own body on the tree,
that we, being dead to sins, should live unto righteousness: by
whose stripes ye were healed.

1 Peter 2:24

Thank you, Lord, for enduring unimaginable pain, even to the point of death, so that my broken relationship with my heavenly Father can be healed. By that healing, may all my emotional wounds be healed as well.

In your name, I pray. Amen.

October 7

Being confident of this very thing, that he which hath begun a good work in you will perform it until the day of Jesus Christ.

Philippians 1:6

*L*ord, help my eyes to see all the ways you are working in this world. Because of your great compassion and active involvement, the effects of everything you accomplish are multiplied many times over. We praise you, Lord, and pray you will continue to be involved in our lives and in our world. And may our deeds and thoughts always honor you.

October 8

Wherefore take unto you the whole armour of God, that ye may be able to withstand in the evil day, and having done all, to stand.

Ephesians 6:13

Lord, be my warrior, my guard, my guide. Let your love be the armor that shields me from the slings and arrows of the day. Let your compassion be the blanket that protects me from the cold at night. Lord, be my champion and protector. Let your love surround me like an impenetrable light that nothing can break through to do me harm. Let your grace bring me peace no matter how crazy things are all around me. Lord, be my warrior.

October 9

He caused an east wind to blow in the heaven: and by his power he brought in the south wind.

Psalm 78:26

All around, leaves are falling, drifting, and swooping in the wind. They become a whirligig, a dance of wind and nature. They are a picture of the heavenly places where lighthearted beings are carried by the invisible power of love.

October 10

But if we walk in the light, as he is in the light, we have fellowship one with another, and the blood of Jesus Christ his Son cleanseth us from all sin.

1 John 1:7

*D*ear God, what joy we have in gathering to pray and praise you together. How encouraging it is to share what's happening on our separate life journeys and see your hand at work in so many different ways. Thank you for arranging those times of fellowship, Lord. They are blessed times indeed.

October 11

He that loveth his brother abideth in the light, and there is none occasion of stumbling in him.

1 John 2:10

Heavenly Father, we are thankful for family. Please bring our family together in happiness. Help us see everything as children do: with wonder and awe. Glorious are your creations! Thank you for creating us. We love our family. We love you. Amen.

October 12

Let the heaven and earth praise him, the seas, and every thing
that moveth therein.

Psalm 69:34

May you celebrate this day with all your heart.

Rejoice in the beauty of its light and warmth.

Give thanks for the air and grass and sidewalks.

Let gratitude for other faces flow into your soul.

And cherish the chance to work and play, to

think and speak—

knowing this: All simple pleasures are

opportunities for praise.

October 13

Hast not thou made an hedge about him, and about his house, and about all that he hath on every side? thou hast blessed the work of his hands, and his substance is increased in the land.

Job 1:10

You invented work, God, and I am grateful. Framer of the cosmos, you've given me a project, too. Creator of earth and oceans, sustain my hands to do it right. Designer of amoebas and atoms, give me pause to look after the details. Worker of ultimate skill, accomplish your masterwork in my soul this day!

October 14

Blessed are the poor in spirit: for theirs is the kingdom of heaven.

Matthew 5:3

Remind us, Lord, that you dwell among the lowliest of people. You are the God of the poor, walking with beggars, making your home with the sick and the unemployed. Keep us mindful always that no matter how much we have, our great calling is to depend on you—for everything, every day of our lives.

October 15

He maketh the storm a calm, so that the waves thereof are still.

Psalm 107:29

Lord, you are my lighthouse,
shining like a beacon
in a raging storm,
guiding my way
through the fog and rough seas.

I set my course on you
with patience, perserverance,
and faith, trusting
that you will help me
reach calmer shores.

October 16

They helped every one his neighbour; and every one said to his brother, Be of good courage.

Isaiah 41:6

I thank you for the healing power of friends and for the positive emotions friendship brings. Thank you for sending companions to me so we can support and encourage one another and share our joys and sorrows. My friends represent for me your presence and friendship here on earth. Please keep them in your care, Father. We need each other, and we need you. Amen.

October 17

So that we may boldly say, The Lord is my helper, and I will not fear what man shall do unto me.

Hebrews 13:6

I know there is so much going on in the world that requires your attention. It's just that sometimes I feel

tension simply getting a grip on me. Sometimes worry clouds my view. This distances me from you and from everything in my life. I pray for the freedom to worry less. I want to simply trust you more.

October 18

My soul thirsteth for God, for the living God: when shall I come and appear before God?

Psalm 42:2

O God, sometimes my days are frantic dashes between have to, ought, and should. Lead me to a porch step or a swing, a chair or a hillside, where I can be restored by sitting, Lord, simply sitting. With you there to meet me, sitting places become prime places for collecting thoughts, not to mention fragmented lives.

October 19

And the Lord, he it is that doth go before thee; he will be with
thee, he will not fail thee, neither forsake thee: fear not,
neither be dismayed.

Deuteronomy 31:8

*L*ord, give me the faith to take the next step, even when I
don't know what lies ahead. Give me the assurance that,
even if I stumble and fall, you'll pick me up and put me
back on the path. And give me the confidence that, even if
I lose faith, you will never lose me.

October 20

A new commandment I give unto you, That ye love one another; as I have loved you, that ye also love one another.

John 13:34

*F*ather in heaven, let me be an angel to someone today. Just as you have blessed my life with people who love and cherish me, let me be a light of love that shines upon someone who needs me. I have received the gift of angels, now allow me to give and be one in return.

October 21

For all have sinned, and come short of the glory of God;
Being justified freely by his grace through the redemption that
is in Christ Jesus.

Romans 3:23–24

We shouldn't seek perfection in our friends, for
we are not perfect. We should look for kindness,
compassion, patience, and humor—in our friends
and in our own hearts.

October 22

And they that be wise shall shine as the brightness of the firmament; and they that turn many to righteousness as the stars for ever and ever.

Daniel 12:3

Let me do what lies clearly at hand, this very minute. Grant me the insight to see that too much planning for the future removes me from the present moment. And this is the only existence, the only calling I have been given— right now to do what is necessary. Nothing more, nothing less. Thus may I use this next moment wisely.

October 23

And when they had prayed, the place was shaken where they were assembled together; and they were all filled with the Holy Ghost, and they spake the word of God with boldness.

Acts 4:31

Time is tight, Lord, and I wonder why I bother to pray. The question is answer enough: I need a relationship where I don't have to bluff and hurry. And when I pray boldly? I offer myself as a possible answer to prayer. No time to waste.

October 24

We toss and turn, God of nighttime peace, making lists of "must do" and "should have done" and wind up feeling unequal to the tasks and sleep-deprived to boot.

Bless us with deep sleep and dreams that reveal us as you see us: beloved, worthy, capable. At dawn, help us see possibilities on our lists.

Each time we yawn today, Lord—for it was a short night—we'll breathe in your restorative presence and exhale worries. Tonight we'll sleep like the sheep of your pasture, for we lie down and rise up in your care, restored, renewed, and rested.

October 25

Today I want to spend time with you, Renewing Spirit.
In fact, I'd like to spend the whole day just
being in your presence.
For this one day I will not worry about the work
I have to do or the goals I want to accomplish.
I will pull back and simply listen for your guidance.
I'm willing to change my life in order to fit your perfect will,
and I ask that you begin that work in my heart, even now.
I'll let go of personal ambition, for now.
I'll loosen my grip on the things I've wanted to
accomplish and the recognition I've craved for so long.
All of this I give over to you.
I'm content to be a servant for now, quiet and
unnoticed, if that is what you desire.
I'm even willing to be misunderstood, if you will only
respond to my sincere prayer for a renewed heart.
Thank you. I need you so much.

October 26

Remembering without ceasing your work of faith, and labour of love, and patience of hope in our Lord Jesus Christ, in the sight of God and our Father.

1 Thessalonians 1:3

Hope says, "No matter how many times I fall, I will stand and start again." For a person of hope is not one who never falls, but one who picks herself up one more time than she falls. Jesus, teach me to place my hope in you.

October 27

Many, O Lord my God, are thy wonderful works which thou hast done, and thy thoughts which are to us-ward: they cannot be reckoned up in order unto thee: if I would declare and speak of them, they are more than can be numbered.

Psalm 40:5

Lord, speak to me through these pages.
Let me hear your gentle words
Come whispering through the ages
And thundering through the world.

Teach me how to please you,
Show me how to live.
Inspire me to praise you
For all the love you give.

October 28

I have blotted out, as a thick cloud, thy transgressions, and, as a cloud, thy sins: return unto me; for I have redeemed thee.

Isaiah 44:22

Tossing leaves onto a fire, we name them as regrets and failures from which we choose to be free. We trust you to redeem even these, our deadest moments. They, like autumn leaves, can make the brightest blaze.

Stir new possibilities into life from the embers; fan the sparks of dreams so that we may become one with your purpose for us. It is the root from which we, leaf and human life, begin.

October 29

Then the disciples, every man according to his ability, determined to send relief unto the brethren which dwelt in Judaea.

Acts 11:29

$\mathcal{F}$ather,

It's easy to say, "Let me know if there's anything I can do." But how much better to peer closer, assess the situation to find what needs doing, and then simply do it. Help me look into a friend's needs instead of waiting to be asked. Help me replace the words I utter so glibly with actions that might matter even more.

Amen.

October 30

---

*Let your light so shine before men, that they may see your
good works, and glorify your Father which is in heaven.*

Matthew 5:16

Some prayers are best left unfinished, God of
abundance, and this will be an ongoing conversation
between us. Each day I discover new gifts you offer
me, and the list of reasons to be thankful grows. As I
accept your gifts and live with them thankfully, guide
me to become a person who shares with others so that
they, too, can live abundantly. May someone,
somewhere, someday say of me, "I am thankful to
have this person in my life."

October 31

He that dwelleth in the secret place of the most High shall abide under the shadow of the Almighty.

Psalm 91:1

Spreading your great branches
Over all who come,
Sheltering humble hearts
From judgment's burning sun.
Here your shade of mercy
Stirs breezes deep within.
In heaven's center planted
We find you once again.

November

November 1

---

*For our conversation is in heaven; from whence also we look
for the Saviour, the Lord Jesus Christ.*

Philippians 3:20

When we grieve for lost loved ones, we grieve for
ourselves. God, let me celebrate those who have gone
home to Heaven, those who now know the full essence of
your true love.

November 2

In that he saith, A new covenant, he hath made the first old. Now
that which decayeth and waxeth old is ready to vanish away.

Hebrews 8:13

Lord, the familiar is disappearing from
neighborhood and nature, and we grieve the loss. Yet,
we're resurrection people, unafraid of endings
because of the promise of beginnings. On the other
hand, we must learn restraint: Help us, God, to
temper our actions with wisdom. Amen.

November 3

The word which God sent unto the children of Israel, preaching peace by Jesus Christ: (he is Lord of all).

Acts 10:36

*L*ove is an active force. When we "walk our talk" and live God's message of love, we create an America full of faith. When we do that, we are God's voice, his hands, his light for each other. We are living love.

November 4

$\mathcal{L}$ord, it is sometimes hard to love those around me when they are so different in their beliefs and behaviors. I find myself sometimes feeling intolerant, even afraid. But you gave me the commandment to love others as myself, and that if I love you, then I love all of your creation. Help me to open my heart and my mind to those I see as being different, and to find in them the common light of your presence. Help me to be a better person and not fear others just because they are not like me. Help me to see the wonder and magic in learning about others and letting them learn about me.

November 5

And now abideth faith, hope, charity, these three; but the greatest of these is charity.

1 Corinthians 13:13

The angel of faith helps us trust God despite our circumstance. The angel of hope helps us press on through our circumstance. But the angel of God's love holds us in our circumstance.

November 6

For I will restore health unto thee, and I will heal thee of thy wounds, saith the Lord; because they called thee an Outcast, saying, This is Zion, whom no man seeketh after.

Jeremiah 30:17

Wondrous God, I praise your name.

Your Word is life.

I believe you can heal me.

Be with me when I am sick, and remind me to praise you

when I am well.

Thank you for healing me in the past,

And for future healing.

Keep me in good health

That I might serve you

And praise your name.

Amen.

November 7

My flesh and my heart faileth: but God is the strength of my
heart, and my portion for ever.

Psalm 73:26

Bless my attempts at success, Lord, though I know
many of them will end in failure.

I pray that you will even bless my failures, for I also know
that never risking is a sure sign of sloth and a questioning
of your constant goodwill toward me.

November 8

For the word of God is quick, and powerful, and sharper than any twoedged sword, piercing even to the dividing asunder of soul and spirit, and of the joints and marrow, and is a discerner of the thoughts and intents of the heart.

Hebrews 4:12

We are, as the Psalmist says, wondrously made. So much so, loving Creator, that by changing our minds we might be able to change our lives. It's the simple power of "as if." Living as if we are going to fail, we often do. Living as if we are going to succeed, we often can. Keep us from being like teams who know the plays but doubt they can run them. Instead, we'll use your amazing gift of attitude, knowing you treat us as if we deserve your promised abundant life.

November 9

My brethren, count it all joy when ye fall into divers temptations;
Knowing this, that the trying of your faith worketh patience.

James 1:2–3

Lord, help me understand that the challenges I am going through serve to empower me. Teach me the wisdom to discern that my trials mold me into something far grander than even I could have imagined. Amen.

November 10

Therefore being justified by faith, we have peace with God
through our Lord Jesus Christ:
By whom also we have access by faith into this grace wherein
we stand, and rejoice in hope of the glory of God.

Romans 5:1–2

Spirit, help me live one day at a time so that I may meet each day's challenges with grace, courage, and hope. Shelter me from the fears of the future and the anguish of the past. Keep my mind and heart focused on the present, where the true gift of happiness and healing is to be found. Amen.

November 11

Have not I commanded thee? Be strong and of a good courage;
be not afraid, neither be thou dismayed: for the Lord thy God
is with thee whithersoever thou goest.

Joshua 1:9

Today I pray for our country and all those who serve in our military. God ignites the stars upon our nation's flag, keeping them shining through sunny celebrations; farewells to heroes; and our long dark nights.

November 12

You created your world as a circle of love, designer God, a wonderful round globe of beauty. And you create us still today in circles of love— families, friendships, communities.

Yet your circle of love is repeatedly broken because of our love of exclusion. We make separate circles: inner circle and outer circle; circle of power and circle of despair; circle of privilege and circle of deprivation. We need your healing touch to smooth our sharp edges. Remind us that only a fully round, hand-joined circle can move freely like a spinning wheel or the globe we call home.

November 13

This is a faithful saying, and worthy of all acceptation, that Christ Jesus came into the world to save sinners; of whom I am chief.

1 Timothy 1:15

Help me, God, to see that you gave your love in such a way that even the most wicked person can repent and find new life in your grace and mercy; indeed, that your love calls even the worst sinners to become your children. You created each person with a specific purpose to serve in this world. Help me, Lord, to pray that each person will turn away from evil, turn to you, and become your devoted servant. Amen.

November 14

Let us hold fast the profession of our faith without wavering;
(for he is faithful that promised).

Hebrews 10:23

*L*ike a speed bump in a parking lot, a decision lies in our path, placed there by God to remind us hope is a choice. Choosing to live as people of hope is not to diminish or belittle pain and suffering or lie about evil's reality. Rather it is to cling to God's promise that he will make all things new.

November 15

And when ye stand praying, forgive, if ye have ought against any: that your Father also which is in heaven may forgive you your trespasses.

Mark 11:25

Father, I need to understand that forgiveness is not dependent on my feelings but rather on a determination of my will. Help me form a few well-chosen words of forgiveness. Amen.

November 16

I will praise thee; for I am fearfully and wonderfully made:
marvellous are thy works; and that my soul knoweth right well.

Psalm 139:14

Bless you, Lord!
The heavens declare your glory;
the skies proclaim your mighty power.
And here I am, looking up into
those vast regions, knowing
that the tiniest cell in my body
is a most glorious miracle, as well.
Bless you, Lord!

November 17

Forgive me for complaining, dear God. Help me to remember that every time I have a headache, someone I know may have a hidden heartache; every time I don't like the food, millions have nothing to eat; every time I think my paycheck is small, too many people have no paycheck at all; every time I wish my loved ones were not so demanding, some people have no

one to love. When I look around at my blessings, my complaints seem little. Teach me perspective, God, and to be grateful for my everyday gifts of family, food, and home. Amen.

November 18

And now the Lord shew kindness and truth unto you: and I also will requite you this kindness, because ye have done this thing.

2 Samuel 2:6

It's hard to be pleasant these rude, road-raging days. Everyone's too immersed in their own concerns to be mannerly or kind. Encourage me to get in the first words of "please," "thanks," and "excuse me"; nudge me to be the first to take turns on the road, in the store, at work. Maybe good manners will be as catching as rude ones; may I, with your guidance, be first to pass them on.

November 19

And to love him with all the heart, and with all the understanding, and with all the soul, and with all the strength, and to love his neighbour as himself, is more than all whole burnt offerings and sacrifices.

Mark 12:33

Bless my neighbor today. But keep me from telling him that I've got his good in mind. Only let him discover in my smile, in my encouraging words, and in my helping hand.

November 20

Withhold not thou thy tender mercies from me, O Lord: let thy lovingkindness and thy truth continually preserve me.

Psalm 40:11

Everything around me keeps changing, Lord. Nothing lasts. My relationships with others are different than they were before. I started to feel as if there is nothing sure and steady on which I can depend. Then I

remembered your ever-present, unchanging love. Through these transitions, your love gives me courage and hope for the future. Amen.

November 21

For the oppression of the poor, for the sighing of the needy, now will I arise, saith the Lord; I will set him in safety from him that puffeth at him.

Psalm 12:5

God, I look around my community today and I feel helpless. The homeless, the hurting, the needs each one represents are more than I can handle. But you can do it. You can meet each need. Teach me. Strengthen me and use me to serve as I reach out to my neighbor and meet Just One Need at a Time!

November 22

———◆———

But thanks be to God, which giveth us the victory through our Lord Jesus Christ.

1 Corinthians 15:57

In all things, give thanks.
In the good days of laughter and joy, give thanks.
In the bad days of struggle and strife, give thanks.
In the brightest moments and the darkest hours, give thanks.
In the flow of blessings and the apparent
lack of goodness, give thanks.
In the face of fortune and misfortune, give thanks.
In the presence of pleasure and pain, give thanks.
In all things, give thanks.
For lessons and blessings are found not just in the light,
but in the darkness.

November 23

Lord, what is man, that thou takest knowledge of him! or the son of man, that thou makest account of him!

Psalm 144:3

Thank you, Lord, for reaching out and drawing me under your wings. Even though I am just one of billions of people who need you, your love is so great that you know my troubles, are concerned for my welfare, and are working to renew my dreams. I am so blessed to have you to turn to when I am faced with a calamity, and I am so very grateful that I have you to lean on. I praise you with all my heart. Amen.

November 24

For the promise you unfold with the opening of each day,
I thank you, Lord.
For blessings shared along the way, I thank you, Lord.
For the comfort of our home filled with love to
keep us warm, I thank you, Lord.
For shelter from the winter storm, I thank you, Lord.
For the gifts of peace and grace you grant the
family snug within, I thank you, Lord.
For shielding us from harm and sin, I thank you, Lord.
For the beauty of the snow sparkling in the
winter sun, I thank you, Lord.
For the peace when the day is done, I thank you, Lord.

November 25

O Lord, we give thanks for your presence, which greets us each day in the guise of a friend, a work of nature, or a story from a stranger. We are reminded through these messengers in our times of deepest need that you are indeed watching over us. Lord, we have known you in the love and care of a friend, who keeps us company in our despair. When we observe the last morning glory stretching faithfully to receive what warmth is left in the chilly sunshine, we are heartened and inspired to do the same. When we are hesitant to speak up and then read in the newspaper a story of courage and controversy, we find our voice lifted and strengthened by your message in black-and-white type. Lord, we are grateful receivers of all the angelic messages that surround us every day.

November 26

To the end that my glory may sing praise to thee, and not be silent. O Lord my God, I will give thanks unto thee for ever.

Psalm 30:12

We thank thee,

O Lord whose finger touched our dust,

O Lord who gave us breath.

We thank thee, Lord, who gave us sight and sense

to see the flower,

to hear the wind,

to feel the waters in our hand,

to sleep with the night and wake with the sun,

to stand upon this star,

to sing thy praise,

to hear thy voice.

November 27

Take heed therefore unto yourselves, and to all the flock, over the which the Holy Ghost hath made you overseers, to feed the church of God, which he hath purchased with his own blood.

Acts 20:28

Lord, today my heart is full of gratitude for your church. Thank you for asking us to meet together to honor you. What power there is in voicing our thanks and petitions together! What comfort in the outstretched arms of friends! Protect us, Lord. Keep us strong—now and in the days to come.

November 28

With him is wisdom and strength,
he hath counsel and understanding.

Job 12:13

God, I give thanks for the wisdom you share with me when I am trying to understand my own actions or someone else's. You know what is best, and you have my highest good in mind. I will turn to you for the advice and guidance I need. Thank you, God, for being a strong and loving presence in my life. Amen.

November 29

Every good gift and every perfect gift is from above, and cometh down from the Father of lights, with whom is no variableness, neither shadow of turning.

James 1:17

How good it is, Almighty One, to bask in the warmth of your love. How good it is to know nothing more is required than this: to receive your good gifts from above.

November 30

For I the Lord thy God will hold thy right hand, saying unto thee, Fear not; I will help thee.

Isaiah 41:13

In silence I kneel in your presence—I bow my heart to your wisdom; I lift my hands for your mercy; I open my soul to the great gift. I am already held in your arms.

December

December 1

These things I have spoken unto you, that in me ye might have peace. In the world ye shall have tribulation: but be of good cheer; I have overcome the world.

John 16:33

Enliven my imagination, God of new life, so that I can see through today's troubles to coming newness. Surround me with your caring so that I can live as if the new has already begun.

December 2

For thou wilt light my candle: the Lord my God
will enlighten my darkness.

Psalm 18:28

I am feeling my way in this darkness, God, and it
seems I'm going in circles. Yet you have reminded me—
quietly, just now—that I am encircled by your love no
matter which way I choose to go.

December 3

For which cause we faint not; but though our outward man perish, yet the inward man is renewed day by day.

2 Corinthians 4:16

Connected in memory to holidays past, like links in a colorful paper chain decorating the tree, we are in the beginning days of another Advent season. Some recollections are happy and pleasant, others sad and empty, yet each brings us to this new starting point, as fresh and full of promise as an egg about to hatch. Make all things new this holiday, even old memories, for this is the season of second chances.

December 4

And he shall go before him in the spirit and power of Elias, to turn the hearts of the fathers to the children, and the disobedient to the wisdom of the just; to make ready a people prepared for the Lord.

Luke 1:17

O Lord, what a blessing to be in the Advent season and prayerfully considering the joyous celebration of your birth. Don't let us get so bogged down by minutiae that we miss the miracle, Lord. Prepare our hearts as we prepare our homes and families for Christmas, and help us keep our focus not on everything we need to do, but on you.

December 5

Now the God of patience and consolation grant you to be likeminded one toward another according to Christ Jesus: That ye may with one mind and one mouth glorify God, even the Father of our Lord Jesus Christ.

Romans 15:5–6

My aim is...
to please him through communing in prayer
to show his love and for others care
to read his Word as my guide for life
to cease my grumbling that causes strife
to be open to God's leading and his will
to take time to meditate, be quiet, and still
to continually grow in my Christlike walk
to be more like Jesus in my life and my talk.

December 6

Depart from evil, and do good; seek peace, and pursue it.

Psalm 34:14

Bless me with a peacemaker's kind heart and a builder's sturdy hand, Lord, for these are mean-spirited, litigious times when we tear down with words and weapons first and ask questions later. Help me take every opportunity to compliment, praise, and applaud as I rebuild peace.

December 7

---

*And straightway the father of the child cried out, and said
with tears, Lord, I believe; help thou mine unbelief.*

Mark 9:24

I need to believe beyond the present darkness, for it
threatens to stop me in my tracks. Steady me, God of
infinite resources, as I collect my beliefs like candles to
light and move through this dark tunnel of doubt and

uncertainty. Inspire me
to add new truths as they
reveal themselves in my
life. Along the way, help
my unbelief.

December 8

Behold, what manner of love the Father hath bestowed upon us, that we should be called the sons of God: therefore the world knoweth us not, because it knew him not.

1 John 3:1

Let your peace rest upon our home, dear God. We do not know how to love one another as you have loved us. We fail to reach out the way you have gathered us in. We forget how to give when only taking fills our minds. And, most of all, we need your presence to know we are more than just parents and children. We are always your beloved sons and daughters here. Let your peace rest upon our home, dear God.

December 9

My little children, let us not love in word, neither in tongue; but in deed and in truth.

1 John 3:18

I wish to extend my love, Lord. So give me hands quick to work on behalf of the weak. Cause my feet to move swiftly in aid of the needy. Let my mouth speak words of encouragement and new life. And give my heart an ever-deepening joy through it all.

December 10

So that contrariwise ye ought rather to forgive him, and comfort him, lest perhaps such a one should be swallowed up with overmuch sorrow.

2 Corinthians 2:7

Father, when we stand to cross the metaphorical bridge of forgiveness, please give us a little push to get us going. Amen.

December 11

Thou madest him a little lower than the angels; thou crownedst him with glory and honour, and didst set him over the works of thy hands:

Hebrews 2:7

With clean hands and a pure heart, may I be worthy to do the work of angels.

December 12

But Jesus beheld them, and said unto them, With men this is impossible; but with God all things are possible.

Matthew 19:26

Only faith can look past a seemingly impossible situation and believe that it will change. I believe you are a God of miracles, Lord. These are days of miracles, as were the days of Noah, Moses, and Joseph. I may not see the seas parted, peoples freed, or congregations caught up to heaven, but through faith I expect wonderful gifts from you. I believe that with you, all things are possible!

December 13

And the King shall answer and say unto them, Verily I say unto you, Inasmuch as ye have done it unto one of the least of these my brethren, ye have done it unto me.

Matthew 25:40

Heavenly Father, when you sent Jesus, you gave your best to us. As I consider how to go about emulating that kind of love, I'd like to give in a significant way to someone who is in need. There are many, many opportunities to give, but I'd like to do more than just buy a present; I'd like to give myself.

December 14

The Lord is my light and my salvation; whom shall I fear? the Lord is the strength of my life; of whom shall I be afraid?

Psalm 27:1

In the midst of the darkness that threatens to overwhelm us lies a pinpoint of light, a persistent flicker that guides us through the pain and fear, through the hopelessness and despair, to a place of peace and healing on the other side. This is God's Spirit, leading us back home like the lighthouse beacon that directs the ships through the fog to the safety of the harbor.

December 15

Let thy mercy, O Lord, be upon us, according as we hope in thee.

Psalm 33:22

*L*ike the evergreen, hope never dies, but stands tall and mighty against the coldest winter winds until the summer sun returns to warm its outstretched branches.

December 16

And I myself also am persuaded of you, my brethren, that ye also are full of goodness, filled with all knowledge, able also to admonish one another.

Romans 15:14

Lord, teach me to emulate your goodness.

December 17

And thou shalt love the Lord thy God with all thine heart, and with all thy soul, and with all thy might.

Deuteronomy 6:5

I know yours is a persistent devotion, Lord. Your devoted love for me is the example that helps me to love others as well. What would I prefer to your love? What could I love more than those I hold dear? Nothing in the universe! Who are the loves of my life? Let me count them all and delight in them today.

December 18

He shall be great, and shall be called the Son of the Highest:
and the Lord God shall give unto him the throne of his father
David: And he shall reign over the house of Jacob for ever; and
of his kingdom there shall be no end.

Luke 1:32–33

You are a welcome guest at this table, God, as we
pause in the midst of this bell-ringing, carol-making
season of too much to do. Send us your gift of silent
nights so that we can hear and know what you will be
bringing us this year: yet another gift of hope. Bless
our gathering around this table; we will set a place
each day for you. Join us in our daily feast, for which
we now give thanks. May it nourish our busy bodies
as the anticipation of your presence among us does
our weary spirits.

December 19

Rejoicing in hope; patient in tribulation; continuing instant in prayer; Distributing to the necessity of saints; given to hospitality.

Romans 12:12–13

*T*angled in tape, lists, and holiday wrappings, we are all thumbs of excitement! Bless the surprises we've selected, wrapped, and hidden. Restore us to the joy of anticipation. We want to be surprised, too. Our wish lists include the gift of peace possibilities, of ears to hear a summons and eyes to spot another's need or triumph, of being able to make a difference. As we cut and tape, God of surprises, remind us to keep in touch with the gift's recipient after the wrapping papers are long gone and the ornaments packed.

December 20

Wait on the Lord: be of good courage, and he shall strengthen thine heart: wait, I say, on the Lord.

Psalm 27:14

God, I am scurrying around like a chicken with its head cut off, making a huge mess everywhere I go. Why, God, when I know I do better and work more efficiently when I wait quietly and listen for your guidance, do I rush about—driven by time rather than by you?

Help me, God, to slow down, to be silent, so I can hear you and do your will, not mine.

December 21

In my Father's house are many mansions: if it were not so, I would have told you. I go to prepare a place for you.

John 14:2

Lord, I'm looking forward to sharing a home with you. Thank you for becoming poor so that I could become rich. Amen.

December 22

While we look not at the things which are seen, but at the things which are not seen: for the things which are seen are temporal; but the things which are not seen are eternal.

2 Corinthians 4:18

In the lights and glimmer of modern Christmas decorations we see a tiny speck of brilliance that is the reality angels see, share, and return to when their task on earth is complete. It's a brilliance we can one day see for ourselves when our task is done as well.

December 23

And Jesus said unto them, Because of your unbelief: for verily I say unto you, If ye have faith as a grain of mustard seed, ye shall say unto this mountain, Remove hence to yonder place; and it shall remove; and nothing shall be impossible unto you.

Matthew 17:20

Into the bleakest winters of our souls, Lord, you are tiptoeing on tiny infant feet to find us. May we drop whatever we're doing and accept this gesture of a baby so small it may get overlooked in our frantic search for something massive and overwhelming. Remind us that it is not you who demands lavish celebrations and strobe-lit displays of faith. Rather, you ask only that we have the faith of a mustard seed and willingness to let a small hand take ours. We are ready.

December 24

The voice of him that crieth in the wilderness, Prepare ye the way
of the Lord, make straight in the desert a highway for our God.

Isaiah 40:3

The Christmas tree, O God, is groaning beneath gift-wrapped anticipation. The table spread before us is resplendent with shared foods prepared by loving hands, for which we give thanks. And now, as this waiting season ticks to a bell-ringing, midnight-marvelous close, we around this table are scooting over to make room for the anticipated Guest. Come, blessing us with the gift of your presence as we say, "Welcome."

December 25

---

*And the angel said unto them, Fear not: for, behold, I bring
you good tidings of great joy, which shall be to all people.
For unto you is born this day in the city of David a Saviour,
which is Christ the Lord.*

Luke 2:10–11

Compassionate and holy God, we celebrate your coming
into this world. We celebrate with hope, we celebrate with
peace, we celebrate with joy. Through your giving our lives
are secure. Through your love we, too, can give love. You
are the source of our being. Joy to our world.

December 26

For unto us a child is born, unto us a son is given: and the government shall be upon his shoulder: and his name shall be called Wonderful, Counsellor, The mighty God, The everlasting Father, The Prince of Peace.

Isaiah 9:6

Lord, how grateful we are that our spirits don't have to sag once the excitement of Christmas is over! We don't want to be like ungrateful children tearing through a pile of presents just to say, "Is that all?" For the gift you gave us at Christmas, your beloved son among us, is a gift that is ours all the days of our lives and throughout eternity! Thank you for the greatest gift of all, Lord.

December 27

And all they that heard it wondered at those things which were
told them by the shepherds.
But Mary kept all these things, and pondered them in her heart.

Luke 2:18–19

Mary delighted in her son. What an honor it was
to have such an intimate connection to Jesus. And
what a wonderful, loving mother Mary was! As she
listened to the amazing things the visiting shepherds
had to say about her precious child, Mary quietly
listened, pondering these things and filing them
away in her heart. May all mothers look to Mary's
example, Lord. May we parent generously and wisely,
gently encouraging our children to look to your plans
for their lives.

December 28

There are three kinds of people in the world: those who give off light, those who give off dark shadows, and those who give off nothing. Lord, help me to be a giver of light, a bearer of hope, a bringer of faith. For only light can dispel the darkness, and only light can brighten deadened places and bring them back to life. Jesus admonished us not to hide our light. We were not meant to cower fearfully amid the shadows or to huddle in dark corners undetected. We were meant to go forth into the world and shine.

December 29

$\mathcal{I}$n this world where human love is conditional and often temporary, it is a joy to know that God loves us unconditionally and eternally. Nothing we can say or do will cause him to stop loving us. Our minds cannot even imagine the immensity of his love for each person on this planet. He sent his son here to deliver that message of love personally. When he died for us, he was saying

through his action, "I love you." God remains always ready to lavish his love on his children. May I open my heart to receive all the love he has to offer.

December 30

For all the gods of the nations are idols:
but the Lord made the heavens.

Psalm 96:5

*L*ord, as I clean out closets and make lists for the New
Year, show me any "gods" I have placed before you.
Help me to look honestly at how I spend my time and
my money. Does one of these areas of investment
reveal a strong allegiance to something other than
you? If so, Lord, help me eradicate those distractions
from my life once and for all.

December 31

O Lord, bless our life stages, for they read like growth rings on a mighty tree: our beginnings and firsts with their excitement, newness, and anxiety; our middles, full of diligence and commitment and, yes, we confess, sometimes boredom, but also risk and derring-do; our "nexts," the harvests and reapings; the slowing down and freedom. In your hands this time can be rich and full like an overflowing cup, not a last or a final or an empty or an ending stage at all. You are an Alpha and Omega God, the parentheses between which we live, move, and have our being. Bless our comings and goings.

PHOTO CREDITS: